Practicing Judicious Discipline:

An Educator's Guide to a Democratic Classroom

Second Edition:
Revised and Expanded

—Edited by Barbara McEwan—

Caddo Gap Press
1994

Practicing Judicious Discipline:
An Educator's Guide to a Democratic Classroom

Edited by **Barbara McEwan**

Second Edition, Revised and Expanded, 1994
First Edition, 1991

Published by
Caddo Gap Press
3145 Geary Boulevard, Suite 275
San Francisco, California 94118

Copyright 1991 and 1994 by Barbara McEwan

Price - $14.95

ISBN 1-880192-09-8

Cover drawing by Brynn Lawler

Contents

Acknowledgements

The greatest pleasure derived from the writing and editing of this book was reviewing the stimulating and exciting ideas developed by all of the contributing authors. Articles and lesson plans submitted for this supplement were developed and written by practicing educators in school districts and institutions of higher education in several states, reflecting their work with *Judicious Discipline* in schools and classrooms. I wish to acknowledge their work and thank them for their contributions.

—Barbara McEwan

Foreword

—By Forrest Gathercoal—

The life of a writer is often a lonely one, due to the nature of the art and the absence of those with whom ideas might be shared. I feel very fortunate, however, that during much of the development of *Judicious Discipline* I had the opportunity to work with Barbara McEwan who so ably edited the first edition. After her initial work on my book, I encouraged her to branch out and create a supplement for *Judicious Discipline* that would reflect the work she and others have done helping me research and test my ideas as well as experimenting with applications of the concepts.

Dr. McEwan, who is on the faculty of the School of Education at Oregon State University, has continued to research effective strategies for implementing these concepts in classrooms and to work closely with many teachers and administrators practicing *Judicious Discipline* in their schools and classrooms. She has integrated the model's concepts with cooperative learning strategies as well as the classroom management methods of Rudolph Dreikurs, William Glasser, and others who advocate a democratic, student-centered approach to discipline. She also travels extensively throughout the United States giving presentations and workshops based upon both *Judicious Discipline* books.

It is with great enthusiasm that I recommend *Practicing Judicious Discipline*. Barbara McEwan has the ability to translate the raw material of principles into a meaningful and workable tool for classroom teachers. It is my hope that the ideas and lesson plans in this book will help educators establish and maintain a democratic environment in schools and classrooms. Only empowered educators are able to empower students with rights and responsibilities necessary to truly value learning from and interacting with others.

Introduction
—By Barbara McEwan—

Tommy's student teacher had just introduced a hands-on activity to the group of fourth graders she had gathered in the school gym. The lesson was designed to encourage cooperation among students by having them work in pairs. While other class members busily got to work, Tommy refused to select a partner and instead was slumped against a wall of the room. Jeannie, the student teacher, responded to Tommy's recalcitrant attitude with frustration. "Tommy," she said, "you have a choice. Either you do this activity or I'm going to give you a test." Tommy shook his head and began to cry. "Ok, Tommy, you made your choice. I'm going to get some work for you."

Jeannie's exasperated response is not unique to teachers new or old who find themselves faced with a power struggle. Often educators perceive such attitudes as stemming from a deliberate attempt by students to disrupt the classroom environment. More often the reality has more to do with the baggage they bring with them and a lack of teacher strategies for handling personal problems.

As students enter classrooms on days when they have experienced a serious disturbance at home, teasing by other children on the way to school, not much sleep the night before, or no breakfast that morning, they are very likely to exhibit any number of behaviors usually considered disruptive. *Judicious Discipline* and many other student-centered approaches to classroom management, on the other hand, offer a way to view Tommy's actions very differently. This alternative perspective advocates the idea that children in our schools are probably not making a conscious choice to misbehave—they are just doing the best they can on a bad day.

The manner in which teachers and administrators respond to such situations is crucial, often making the difference between a confrontation that escalates into an angry exchange or a private conversation that can be the first step in a healing process. If students are consumed with the never-ending challenge of trying to draw a teacher's attention to their singular needs, the volition to behave cooperatively is lost. Many schools have a clearly-defined set of administrative rules, complete with punitive responses, geared to any deviant behavior. In the case of some students, this is the one aspect of education they experience most often. The subsequent discouragement and disenfranchisement they inevitably experience leaves them perceiving educators as being unfair and inconsistent.

Compelled into public classrooms they believe to be governed capriciously, students will attempt to attain some personal control over their situation by challenging the system and, all too often, hurting themselves irreparably in the process. The prospect for preserving the fragile self-esteem of students rests on what teachers believe to be their role as professional educators in the classroom.

If teachers presuppose that demanding respect and controlling behaviors is of primary importance in a well-managed classroom, punishing a child who is having a bad day may seem to be a reasonable strategy. On the other hand, teachers who accept the idea that self-esteem must be nurtured if learning is to occur take an entirely different approach with a difficult student. Counseling and providing opportunities to make reparations will be crucial components of student-centered discipline policies for teachers who want to help troubled students recover from problems.

Dealing with disruptions in ways that will solve the problem calmly and leave everyone's self-respect intact is what *Judicious Discipline* is all about. This model advocates a synthesis of democratic principles, sound educational practice, and ethics—placing its primary emphasis on the rights of students to their equal opportunity for an education. *Judicious Discipline* is designed to help educators focus their teaching strategies on motivation, encouragement, and building positive self-concepts in order to facilitate learning. It is also designed to provide teachers with guidelines to understand when it's time to intercede and when it's appropriate to back off and allow an opportunity for everyone to just cool down.

A Quick Overview

Judicious Discipline teaches individual rights, as guaranteed by the Constitution, and how those rights are always being balanced against the compelling state interests that protect our society's need for a safe, healthy, and undisrupted environment. Teachers using *Judicious Discipline* in their classrooms begin by introducing students to the rights guaranteed to citizens under the First, Fourth, and Fourteenth Amendments. This is followed by an explanation of when those rights can and should be taken away. If a teacher, administrator, or staff member is able to demonstrate that the actions of students pose a threat to the health and safety, property, and/or educational purpose of the school, then students should have restrictions placed upon their freedoms.

What makes *Judicious Discipline* unique is the constitutional language used to address problems. When the language of citizenship rights and responsibilities is used to mediate problems between students and teachers, the classroom is transformed into a participatory democratic community.

This constitutional foundation for rules and decision making distinguishes *Judicious Discipline* from other discipline models currently available. In current practice, the most common model employed in school and classroom discipline incorporates the idea that the teacher's right to teach shall not be interfered with by a student who is choosing to misbehave. *Judicious Discipline*, on the other hand, places its emphasis on the concept that it is an educator's professional responsibility to work with and teach every student. Rather than creating an arbitrary set of consequences that apply to any number of inappropriate behaviors, *Judicious Discipline* advocates approaching discipline problems as teachable moments. What does the student need to learn in order to avoid repeating the inappropriate behavior next time? What information does the teacher need to best help the student?

Certainly there are other discipline models that subscribe to democratic practices. Rudolf Dreikurs, William Glasser, Thomas Gordon, and Thomas Lickona, each cited in *Judicious Discipline*, all discuss a variety of democratic strategies such as class meetings, problem solving, and other ideas that empower students to make their own good decisions. *Judicious Discipline* represents a unique addition to this group, because it specifically sets out the legal framework for the decision-making process rather than leaving to chance an understanding of constitutional rights and responsibilities.

Judicious Discipline is not designed to supplant other discipline models, but can be used most successfully in conjunction with any other student-centered approach educators have developed. It provides teachers and administrators with a legal and theoretical framework for making school and classroom decisions as they set about building a democratic learning environment.

For *Judicious Discipline* to be effectively employed at a variety of educational levels in a variety of demographic settings, it must be viewed from a more global perspective. To approach the concepts of constitutional rights and responsibilities from a "how do we use this to control kids" point of view is to severely limit the possibilities of what might occur in an educational environment that celebrates an individual's sense of social responsibility. The essence of *Judicious Discipline* is the appreciation of each student as a human being with diverse needs and abilities. While some students are more difficult to reach than others, given the challenging circumstances from which they come, *Judicious Discipline* firmly maintains that professional educators must never give up trying. Success may not always accompany our efforts, nevertheless professional ethics dictate the need to support and encourage even the most troubled young person.

How This Book Can Help

Deciding how a classroom will operate, what strategies will be used, and what discipline concepts will be employed are all major decisions to be made by teachers as they structure their school year. This supplement is designed to give educators practical ideas for lesson plans, advice from educators who use *Judicious Discipline*, and a compendium of strategies designed to assist in the creation of a school-wide democratic learning environment.

The first part of the book presents a variety of articles dealing with all aspects of building democratic learning environments. The second part is a series of lesson plans written by a number of educators representing all grade levels. The lesson plans have been tested, sometimes reworked, and ultimately found to be successful. The contributing authors of this supplement present you with ideas for encouraging students to work together, teach each other, and enjoy the experience of learning in a democratic classroom.

Conclusion

In the final analysis, *Judicious Discipline* is all about helping educators convey to students that they have permanent value as citizens in the classroom. Recalling the opening scenario between Jeannie and Tommy, how would a teacher using *Judicious Discipline* respond to the behaviors of a recalcitrant student? As Jeannie's supervisor, I advised her to back off and leave Tommy alone until he could pull himself together. She balked at first, fearing that her other students might follow Tommy's example. I pointed out to her that the rest of the class was happily on task, and encouraged her to try leaving Tommy alone for a while to see what might happen.

When I returned to the room later, Tommy was standing up and struggling to pick up some of Jeannie's books that were lying around. I asked if I could help him. "Nope," he said proudly, "I can do it all by myself." As I stood watching him walk slowly down the hall, Jeannie came up beside me. She told me that after Tommy had been given a few minutes to feel better, he had "really gotten into the lesson." She was smiling and very pleased with how things had worked out. Jeannie had learned a basic lesson from *Judicious Discipline*; understanding the importance of maintaining a balance between the rights of one student and her responsibilities to the rest of the class. In addition, she understood that the way we treat one troubled individual sends all of our students a message as to how they will be treated when they too are having a bad day.

Part One

Discussing Judicious Discipline

An Overview
to the Democratic Classroom
—By Richard Jensen—

To possess virtue does not signify having a few nameable traits, it means to be fully and adequately what one is capable of becoming through association with others in all the offices of life.

—John Dewey

When I began my teaching career, I believed that the most practical way to manage a classroom was to posture myself as a Benevolent Dictator, imitating a model with which I had grown up. But in the early 1960s, I returned to school to study counseling and, during that time, became very interested in methods used to guide classroom interactions. My professor proved to be an eloquent advocate of Dreikurs and Adlerian psychology. In particular, I vividly remember a lecture on the concept of freedom, during which he turned to the chalkboard and wrote in capital letters "ESTABLISH ORDER." At first that statement seemed incongruous to me, but as the discussion continued I realized that order is necessary for defining freedom. In other words, without order there would be no concept of freedom. Order provides structure and security, while freedom provides flexibility. Every student and every classroom needs both order and freedom.

In general, three classical forms for establishing order have been identified, and typically the first that springs to mind is order without freedom. Decisions are made with little or no participant input, rules are carried out, and "Because I said so" is the only explanation needed. My metamorphosis from benevolent dictator to democratic teacher occurred in large part because it was pointed out to me that the key word in the first phrase is not benevolent but rather dictator. Most troublesome to me professionally is that this approach does not require students to make decisions about their own behavior.

A second approach, anarchy and permissiveness, particularly as practiced in some educational settings during the 1960s and 1970s, overlooks group responsibility in favor of the students doing their own thing. However child-centered this may appear, it nevertheless has drawbacks. One of my favorite cartoons gives a delightful insight to the tyranny of anarchy. Two Kindergarten children, with sad and pensive expressions on their faces, ask their teacher, "Do we have to do whatever we want to do today?"

The third form, democracy, is defined as freedom with order. This is a classical definition, and one that most of us have not experienced in our own education. The key to establishing order in a democratic classroom is to achieve a balance between freedom and responsibility. The democratic approach is based upon equal worth. Each individual is responsible to self and to others. The benevolent dictator is replaced by a responsive educator, and the student becomes a citizen and an active participant in the learning process.

There are a number of well-known and highly respected educators who have championed the cause of Democratic education. Among them are John Dewey, Thomas Gordon,

William Glasser, and Rudolph Dreikurs. John Dewey believed that to teach democratically meant to respect the student and oneself. Educators should take students as they are, and provide them with experiences to encourage responsible behavior. Meaning and relevancy constitute education as opposed to activity for the sake of activity.

Dreikurs, in *Psychology in the Classroom*, contrasted the two approaches by illustrating the feelings each can engender. As I encourage my students to become Democratic teachers, I find the following list to be a useful reference:

Autocratic Versus Democratic

Autocratic	Democratic
Boss	Leader
Voice, sharp	Voice, friendly
Command	Invitation
Power	Influence
Pressure	Stimulation
Demanding cooperation	Winning cooperation
I tell you what to do	I tell you what I will do
Imposing ideas	Selling ideas
Domination	Guidance
Criticism	Encouragement
Faultfinding	Acknowledging achievement
Punishing	Helping
I tell you	Discussion
I decide, you obey	I suggest, help you decide
Sole responsibility	Shared responsibility

The first column illustrates pressure from without, while the second represents a manifestation of stimulation from within. The two lists set out fundamental differences in beliefs about classroom management and, when examined, permit all teachers to evaluate their own "democratic index."

When Forrest Gathercoal asked me for my reaction to *Judicious Discipline*, the first words that came to mind were: "Your book has made Dreikurs legal." It is rewarding to read a book that will give teachers a firm foundation and clear guidelines for establishing Democratic classrooms.

Making Sense of Whole Language and Judicious Discipline

—By Ken Winograd—

Whole language is a learning theory that effectively informs pedagogical decisions about the teaching of all academic subjects. Once whole language is adopted, teaches often find other ways to infuse democratic practices into their classrooms, including incorporating a system of management that reflects student empowerment. *Judicious Discipline* and whole language share several important assumptions about teaching and learning that combine to support democratic practices.

What is Whole Language?

Whole language is a theory about how people learn oral and written language. Whole language teachers understand that language, as it exists in the real world, represents meaning and is a tool to serve the practical, social needs of people to solve problems, to communicate with others, and to share experiences. Similarly, whole language classrooms promote language activity that serves the practical needs of students to solve real problems, share experiences, etc. In whole language classrooms, for example, students would write and talk to each other in order to reflect upon and learn about the social and scientific world (Edelsky, 1991).

As learners have experiences, they form explanatory hypotheses, test those hypotheses, modify earlier hypotheses, then test again, revise, and so on. Learners here are viewed as active constructors of knowledge, with natural tendencies to raise problems and questions reflecting their everyday experiences. Whole language educators show students how to find the answers to their own questions: in reading and writing, but also in science, social studies, and mathematics.

Whole language teachers understand that children learn best in a context of naturally-occurring social activity. Outside school, adults and children typically engage in joint activity supported by oral and written language. In this context of purposeful and natural activity, all children learn to speak quite well without the benefit of formal language instruction. Children's early language approximations, or mistakes, are accepted (if not valued) as meaningful and sensible. In fact, children's language approximations are indispensable to further development. This is why whole language teachers accept young childrens' invented spellings as a natural stage of writing development.

Whole language teachers believe that one condition of educational activity is that, on surface, it is recognizable in an everyday sense and resembles how people engage in that activity outside school. So students learn to read by reading as people read outside school, learn to write by writing as people write outside school, learn science by doing science as scientists do, learn history by reading and writing history as historians do, etc. One advantage of this conception of school activity as authentic is that it has greater immediate relevance to students than skills-based activity in decontextualized "part language" programs.

Finally, whole language is fundamentally a political movement (Edelsky, 1992; Hoffman, 1992). Whole language is about the empowerment of students and teachers to construct the curriculum together from a shared experience that reflects the local conditions of individual students, teachers, classrooms, and school communities. It is political at the intimate level of reader-text interactions and at the larger level of teacher-student collaboration in the development of the curriculum. Since everyone brings different backgrounds to any text, we can no longer simplistically subscribe to one right meaning, or to one "privileged official interpretation" (Edelsky, 1992). Now, instead of looking primarily to textbook authors or testmakers, the meanings that students bring to experience will reflect their interactions with their literacy communities, such as classrooms, schools, and neighborhoods. At the larger level, whole language means that majority control over school and classroom activity is in the hands of those who actually live in schools—teachers, students, and administrators.

What is *Judicious Discipline*?

The goal of *Judicious Discipline* is to teach students to be citizens in a democracy by having them live in classrooms that are organized democratically. In a *Judicious Discipline* classroom, for example, students would have the right to participate in selecting reading materials and writing topics.

Along with rights comes responsibilities, as in any democratic government. The state (school) has the responsibility to limit student rights for the greater good of the larger student body. This balance on personal rights is embodied in the legal concepts of compelling state interests, meaning the government or school establishes rules that protect the common welfare. In schools, laws come in the form of curricula, academic standards, rules, and schedules.

Legitimate educational purpose relates to the curricular goals, objectives, and activities generated by teachers and school districts. For example, legitimate educational interest supports the teacher's rights to have a math period everyday. However, it is incumbent that the teacher be able to explain, in ways that are understandable to all students, the educational rationale for math as well as all other activity.

A second feature of *Judicious Discipline* is a standard of professional ethics that guides teacher/student relationships. Educators serve as "mentors," facilitating problem resolution where there are violations of classroom rules. When upon to mediate imbalances between student rights and "state interests," students must trust that teachers are going to act in their best interests.

This ethical standard sets the criteria for a "professional relationship" between teacher and student, one that is modeled after that of doctor and patient or lawyer and client. In this relationship, the professional typically opens discussions with probing, exploratory questions such as, "What can I do for you?," "How can I help you?," "What is the problem?" At this point, both parties engage in an open exchange aimed at solving a mutually-understood problem. In the classroom, a professional relationship between teacher and student begins with the same questions. The task for an educator, like that of the doctor or lawyer, is to understand the causes underlying student problems or situations and then work with students to solve them. Like patients or clients, students maintain ownership of the problem, and the teacher, relating as a professional, helps them organize strategies to solve it.

Whole Language and *Judicious Discipline*: Common Ground

Whole language and *Judicious Discipline* both embrace strategies built upon the idea of authenticity. Whole language insists on school literacy activity that is purposeful, meaningful, and resembling literacy activity as it exists outside the school. If students are going to become critical and creative readers and writers, they must participate regularly in authentic language activity by reading, writing, and critiquing authentic text materials. Similarly, *Judicious Discipline* uses an authentic classroom governance structure that is modeled after the United States Constitution.

Judicious Discipline supports the teacher's professional judgment to establish curriculum, organize activities, and, in general, make instructional decisions. However, it is important that the teacher explain curricular decisions to students by going beyond the simple statement "We have to do this activity" and explain that it has a "legitimate educational purpose." Here is an example of one third-grade teacher explaining the education purpose of a lesson on prefixes:

> Girls and boys, we learn about prefixes because they can help us understand unfamiliar words when we're reading. We've all practiced the technique of guess and go: predicting what the word might mean, reading on and then going back to test our prediction. Well, sometimes that technique doesn't help us. So then what we try to do is pick the word apart and see if we can understand any of those parts. Remember, a few weeks ago we learned about base words, and how they can help us make sense of unfamiliar words. Having knowledge of prefixes can also help us "attack" words better.

In both whole language and *Judicious Discipline*, teachers are empowered to make educational decisions that are based on their moral, intellectual, and professional understandings. However, the trust that both models place in teachers to make intelligent educational decisions is in sharp contrast to other, more prevailing, management and curricular programs, such as many basal reading series and "Assertive Discipline." Whole language and *Judicious Discipline* recognize and value the meanings students bring to the educational experience.

In one fourth-grade class, the teacher noticed that many of the students' stories did not contain adequate description to help the reader understand the setting or the characters. In response, the teacher read several very descriptive sections from *Island of the Blue Dolphins*, leading the students to analyze how Scott O'Dell formed his words to create rich descriptions. The students suggested that they record, on butcher paper, a list of interesting descriptive phrases used by O'Dell. So the teacher read the selection again, and the students directed the teacher when to jot a phrase on the paper. The students discussed how they could use models of descriptive writing from their favorite trade books as models in their own writing.

Certainly, teachers make more intelligent instructional decisions when they understand how their students make sense of the world. Whole language and *Judicious Discipline* teachers patiently observe and talk with their students. Here is a journal entry of a teacher-researcher, describing her observations of a third-grade student who, on the surface, appeared to be having problems with a writing task:

> Steven sits at desk, pencil in hand, paper is blank. He stares off into space for five minutes, talks to his neighbor about recess. He writes four words, stops, gets up and walks around room. I wait to see what he does. He walks

the long way to pencil sharpener. Then he takes long way back looking over shoulder of other students writing. Steven sits down and begins writing. In four minutes, he's produced a page of writing. It appears that his walking about the room somehow helped Steven come up with ideas for writing. Maybe this kid's a kinesthetic learner.

Finally, in *Judicious Discipline* and whole language, there is a natural connection between activity and outcome, behavior and consequence. In Melinda Michaels' fifth grade, when students write a story, the evaluation is based on the students' goal for the piece. If the student's goal is to capture a particular mood or emotion, and have the audience respond accordingly, one criterion for evaluating the piece is how the audience actually responds to that piece. In *Judicious Discipline*, if a student hurts someone's feelings in class, the consequence might be for the student to participate in determining how best to recover from the problem. The success of the solution will be determined by how well the two students are able to work together in the future.

The intrinsic relationship between activity/goal and behavior/consequence, typical of whole language and *Judicious Discipline*, I believe, can only serve to make the curriculum more rational to students.

Conclusion

Whole language and *Judicious Discipline* empower teachers and students to find the answers to their own questions. Because the questions raised in whole language and *Judicious Discipline* classrooms are controlled by teachers and students, both reflect democratic approaches to education that, taken together, are theoretically coherent and compatible. For teachers who conceive of schools and classrooms as laboratories for democracy, these two models are certainly worthy of examination. Together they make sense.

References & Sources

Edelsky, C. (1991). A critical component in content study. In J. Hydrick (Ed.), *Whole language: Empowerment at the chalkface*, (pp. 221-219). New York: Scholastic.

Edelsky, C. (1992). A talk with Carol Edelsky about politics and literacy. *Language Arts*, 69, pp. 324-329.

Edelsky, C., Altwerger, B., & Flores, B. (1991). *Whole language: What's the difference?* Portsmouth, NH: Heinemann.

Gathercoal, F. (1993). *Judicious discipline*, 3rd ed. San Francisco, CA: Caddo Gap Press.

Goodman, K. (1986). *What whole in whole language?* Portsmouth, NH: Heinemann.

Hoffman, J. V. (1992). Leadership in the language arts: Am I whole yet? Are you? *Language Arts*, 69, pp. 366-371.

McEwan, B., (Ed.) (1991). *Practicing judicious discipline: An educator's guide to a democratic classroom*, 1st ed. San Francisco, CA: Caddo Gap Press.

The Case for Alternative Assessments

—By Karen M. Higgins—

A man who has left his room in order finds it upon his return in a state of confusion, articles being scattered at random. Automatically, the notion comes to his mind that burglary would account for the disorder. He has not seen the burglars; their presence is not a fact of observation; it is a thought, an idea. The state of the room is a fact, certain, speaking for itself; the presence of burglars is a possibility that may explain the facts. Moreover, the man has no special burglar in mind. The state of his room is perceived and is particular definite - exactly as it is; a burglar is inferred. But no particular individual is thought of; merely some indefinite, unspecified, member of a class.

The original fact, the room as it is first observed, does not by any means **prove** the fact of burglary. The latter conjecture may be correct, but evidence to justify accepting it positively is lacking. The total "fact" as given contains both too much and too little; too much because there are many feature in it that are irrelevant to inference, that are therefore **logically** superfluous. Too little, because the considerations that are crucial—that, if they were ascertained, would be decisive—do not appear on the surface. Thoughtful search for the **kind** of facts that are clues is therefore necessitated. If the illustration were followed out beyond the judgment as to whether there had been a burglary to the question of who the criminal was and how he was to be discovered and the crime brought home to him, the need for extensive and careful examination of the fact side of the case would be even clearer.

This search needs guidance. If it is conducted purely at random a multitude of facts will be turned up, but they will be so unrelated that their very number will add to the difficulty of the case. It is quite possible for thinking to be swamped by the mere multiplicity and diversity of facts. The real problem is: What facts are **evidence** in the case? The search for evidential facts is best conducted when some suggested **possible** meaning is used as a guide in exploring facts, especially in instituting a hunt for some fact that would point conclusively to one explanation and exclude all others. (Dewey, 1933, pp.166-168)

So what does this 1933 quote from Dewey have to do with assessment practices today in a democratic classroom? Many state legislators, curriculum specialists, and teachers, just to name a few of the interested parties, have jumped on the bandwagon of "authentic assessment" or "alternative forms of assessment." Without careful consideration, these forms of assessment, such as portfolios and performance tasks, often become a burden to many teachers in the classroom, thus considered "logically superfluous." According to Roberta Flexer (1992), classroom teachers were involved in the administration and scoring of the assessments done in almost all of the ten states which have incorporated high stakes performance assessments into their states' evaluation processes. On the other hand, many state administrators view learning about and implementing these techniques as instructive for teachers and opportunities for staff development, thus considered a "thoughtful search." What makes these strategies a burden is that many teachers see them as simply an add-on to the assessment practices they are already conducting in the classroom. Adding more to a teacher's already busy schedule and reporting practices would make any teacher cringe at the mere thought of using some of these other assessment alternatives.

Weeding out the superfluous and using meaning to guide the exploration of teachers' assessment practices is the key to sound assessment—in any classroom. Without this meaning, the potential of using more authentic forms of assessment to bring about educational change and reform will never be actualized. So, what guides this process, and how do we balance the "too much" with the "too little?"

Step One: Defining the Case

Teachers need to engage in self-reflection on valued student outcomes.

The first step in creating an assessment system is for teachers to engage in self-reflection on the student outcomes they value within their own classrooms. This process of self-reflection and analysis is perhaps the most important one in establishing meaning for the assessment process. Very often, these outcomes surpass those which are traditionally measured through typical paper/pencil assessments. Many teachers in a democratic classroom view outcomes such as the ability to work with others, honoring other's opinions without being negatively critical, positive self-concept, and self-monitoring, to be as important within the classroom as the discrete content knowledge pertinent to specific curricula areas. However, very often, teachers' assessments only provide information on discrete facts or procedural knowledge—a very small part of what many teachers and other curriculum leaders view to be important goals for teaching and learning.

For an example of educational goals that go beyond traditional measures, we can turn to the National Council of Teachers of Mathematics (1989). The NCTM has advocated five educational goals for students that they believe reflect the importance of mathematical literacy. These goals are the following:

1. Students learning to value mathematics,
2. Students becoming confident in their ability to do mathematics,
3. Students becoming mathematical problem solvers,
4. Students learning to communicate mathematically, and
5. Students learning to reason mathematically. (pp. 5-6)

If mathematics educators expect to help students achieve these goals, their assessment strategies must expand in scope and focus. The ways teachers have traditionally assessed students are simply inadequate for providing information regarding growth in these goals. Mathematics teachers need to design an assessment program for their students that informs all interested parties about progress in some of these very important goals.

Many states around the country have already started implementing major changes in their testing and assessment methods because of documents such as the NCTM *Standards*. Performance assessments, portfolios, open-ended problems, projects, and assessment rubrics, are just a few of the changes taking place. The point is that many factors important to teachers in a democratic classroom can **only** be taken into consideration through some of these other assessment methods. For teachers' assessments to be meaningful, they must align more closely to valued outcomes.

Step Two: Establishing the Facts Which Will Provide Evidence for the Case

Teachers need to align assessment strategies to valued outcomes.

The search for relevant assessment data needs guidance, indeed. What is often missing, as Dewey so explicitly states, is the real problem: "What facts are evidence in this case?" (1933, p. 168). Once the outcomes have been identified, teachers need to consider the full range of assessment strategies at their disposal. Teachers' assessments must be comprehensive and give recognition to all valued learning experiences. This is the reason why the teacher's self-reflection on valued outcomes is so important and why it should be at the heart of all classroom assessment practices. These outcomes guide the teacher towards looking for and compiling the "facts" necessary to provide evidence for reporting valid, pertinent, and meaningful assessment information to all interested parties.

It is important to keep in mind that it is through their assessment practices that teachers communicate most clearly to students which activities and learning outcomes they value. If teachers have created a socially interactive classroom with students involved in cooperative learning, authentic projects, and open-ended problem solving, but when it comes time to assess them teachers distribute the pre-made tests that come with the textbook series, then the message is real clear to students. All that other "stuff" was nice, but that pre-made test is what **truly** matters. It certainly doesn't take students long to figure that one out! If importance is placed on group work and reflection, solving relevant problems, writing across the disciplines, and dispositions about each other as well as the content area, then teachers' assessments should include these components. It is important not to move the target on students by teaching one way and assessing another.

Step Three: The Search for Evidential Facts

Teachers should consider a full range of assessment strategies.

The majority of classroom assessments focus on the end result—the final product, project, or collective sum of knowledge in a certain area. But teachers' assessments can take many forms and happen throughout the learning cycle. As teachers gather the evidence necessary to provide information regarding valued learning outcomes, they should consider three main types of assessment information: process, self-assessment, and product.

Process Information is information collected by the teacher, formally or informally, while students are working. Process information answers questions about students such as: What skills and background knowledge are they bringing to the activity? Are there any surprises to the teacher? Are there deficiencies in background knowledge/skills that may or does interfere with their ability to be successful with the activity? What roles do they assume when working in groups? How well do they work with their peers? How do they interact with their peers? How do they resolve conflicts? Do they tend to prefer working alone? Are there specific things the teacher needs to look for evidence of as they work independently or in groups? Are there specific process questions (i.e., How did you come to this conclusion about the character in your story? What were you thinking when you wrote this part of the problem?) the teacher would like to probe his/her students about?

Process information can be gathered in many ways. Here are a few examples which can be utilized in the classroom:

Checklist with specific items teachers are looking for (pre-determined) and can mark off when they see evidence of the item while students are working independently or in groups.

Computer address labels and/or post-its where the teachers can jot down aberrations and insights about their students. These must be dated and can later be transferred to individual folders or recording sheets. This information can also be xeroxed and shared with parents.

Blank checklists where teachers can record information as the need arises.

Interviews of students regarding the processes they have used; this interview can always be tape-recorded. Process information can also be captured through video taping.

Self-Assessment Information is information students share with teachers that is an assessment of dispositions and abilities. "The capability and willingness to assess their own progress and learning is one of the greatest gifts students can develop. Those who are able to review their own performance, explain the reasons for choosing the processes they used, and identify the next step have a life-long head start" (Stenmark, 1989, p. 26).

There are many purposes for student self-assessment. If students have an opportunity to give regular feedback to teachers regarding problems, anxieties, and areas of needed assistance, then students become partners with teachers in the learning process. Self-assessment can lead to negotiated instruction since it facilitates student-teacher dialogue and student reflection on learning.

Self-assessment information answers questions often asked by the teacher regarding specific feedback on the teaching/learning process. Some examples of questions are: What have I learned about...? How do I feel about...? How well did I work with my group today? What did I contribute? Did I stay involved? What are my strengths and weaknesses? What am I still unsure about? What do I need more help with? How do I know I understand...? How would I explain it to someone else? What types of learning activities do I enjoy the most and feel most comfortable with? What grade do I think I am getting and why?

Some examples of ways to gather self-assessment information include:

Journal entries which can have various degrees of structure;
Autobiographies;
Self-assessment questionnaires which focus students' self-assessment responses;
Learning logs;
Writing assignments (1-2 questions) which focus on self-assessment;
Interviews;
Portfolios which contain student self-selection sections and reasons why students chose particular pieces.

Product Assessment is a student's opportunity to pull together and demonstrate his/her knowledge in some form. It is often a culminating activity and usually answers the question, "How can I best demonstrate what I know?"

As in the other two categories of assessment, there are many ways to gather this information. Here are some examples:

Projects;
Performance tasks;
Traditional paper & pencil tests;
Portfolio of work;
Essay questions;
Knowledge webs;
Reports.

All types of product assessments, no matter what form they take, should have a focused assessment component with, if possible, pre-determined assessment criteria that is explicitly known by the students. Items can simply be marked right or wrong, such as with a traditional paper and pencil test, or scored in more non-traditional ways such as with an analytic or holistic scoring rubric.

Step Four: Establishing the Criteria

Teachers need to collaborate with their students in designing and establishing assessment criteria.

In a democratic classroom, the teacher and his/her students are accustomed to functioning as a community that works collaboratively on classroom rules and other decisions that affect them all. Following this philosophy, it is only natural that students should be empowered to have a say in the criteria with which they will be assessed—individually or as a group. This ownership will improve the quality of all assessment tasks and is an important part of the assessment process often left out in many classrooms.

Although teachers may question whether or not their students are capable of making these types of decisions, they find themselves pleasantly surprised once they facilitate discussions around assessment criteria issues. Not only do students have a sound understanding of criteria relevant to various assessment tasks, they have an uncanny knowledge about their own strengths and weaknesses and often come up with creative and meaningful dimensions for the assessment and evaluation of their own projects and tasks.

One way to begin this discussion is to bring various exemplars of projects into the classroom. In groups of 2-4, students should spend approximately half an hour perusing the projects which have been laid out on the desks around the classroom. Groups' discussions should center on what they like/do not like about the projects as well as what makes them good/not so good. (To maintain confidentiality, names of students should not be on the projects.)

Following this exploration, a teacher-led discussion should focus on the following questions: Which projects were your favorites and why? What makes a good project? What makes a project not so good? Having just witnessed a group of forty first and second graders go through the process, I am convinced of the potential in using this approach as a first step in student-established assessment criteria!

Step Five: Presenting the Case

Teachers should communicate learning gains to students and other interested parties.

It is important to keep in mind that numbers, or letters, do **not** have to be assigned as a final grade on the project/product. But, if these techniques are used for assessment purposes, teachers need to somehow communicate the learning gains their students have made to their students and other interested parties—even if it is just a written narrative which addresses the established assessment criteria. An effective classroom assessment system incorporates strategies which gather information for reasons other than just the evaluation and comparison of students. This balance is important. The documentation and reporting of this information is what gives most teachers' assessments the credibility they deserve.

As teachers move into using assessments for purposes of evaluation, (i.e., grades) a basic tenet is important to keep in mind in a democratic classroom—achievement grades and behavior grades should be kept separate. Especially with high school students, misrepresenting student achievement affects students' Fourteenth Amendment liberty interests, especially because this information is often used by others to decide opportunities for scholarships, admission to classes or colleges, and job perspectives (Gathercoal, 1990).

Step Six: The Closing Remarks

"The proposition that 'all people are created equal,' has never meant that we all possess the same abilities, interests, or talents." (Gathercoal, 1990, p. 7)

Designing an assessment system that takes this important fact into account and balances the individual's abilities with those of her/his classmates may lie at the crux of many assessment issues. This delicate balance is a philosophical underpinning, though, of a democratic classroom. Therefore, incorporating assessments that are consistent with this philosophy rather than counter to it is a challenging, necessary, and exciting prospect. This is especially true since many students view assessments as judgment gavels hanging over their heads—gavels which can descend sternly via the subjective whims of their teachers. In most classrooms, assessments and the criteria for evaluations are often imposed on students rather than negotiated with them.

The value to both students and teachers as they go through this process together is a priceless outcome with many important implications in the classroom. Some implications of using alternative assessment practices include:

> Discourse among students about their thinking.
> Emphasis on understanding concepts.
> Opportunities for student reflection.
> Richer and more meaningful information to share with parents, administrators, and the public.
> Teachers making decisions about instruction based on a broad range of information about student understandings.
> **And**...perhaps the most important...assessments that do not interrupt student learning, but enhance it!

Remember, reliance on only one or two forms of assessment can limit and restrict what you learn about your students and what they can learn about themselves. (Higgins, 1992, p. 10)

Step Six: The Jury's Final Verdict

Teachers have been found guilty of using alternative assessment practices in their

classrooms.

"By following some of these assessment ideas, we pronounce you guilty of tailoring instruction to best meet the needs of your students and using assessment as a powerful tool to improve learning!"

References

Dewey, J. (1933). *How we think. A restatement of the relation of reflective thinking to the educative process.* San Francisco, CA: D.C. Heath and Company.

Flexer, R.J. (1992). "Alternative assessment in mathematics—The action in the states. Who's Doing what?" Paper presented at the annual meeting of the American Educational Research Association, San Francisco, CA.

Gathercoal, F. (1993, 3rd Edition). *Judicious discipline.* San Francisco, CA: Caddo Gap Press.

Higgins, K. (1992). *Classroom assessment training program: Assessing mathematical power.* Portland, OR: NW Regional Educational Laboratory.

National Council of Teachers of Mathematics. (1989). *Curriculum and evaluation standards.* Reston, VA: National Council of Teachers of Mathematics.

Stenmark, J., EQUALS staff, & California Mathematics Council. (1989). *Assessment alternatives in mathematics: An overview of assessment techniques that promote learning.* Berkeley, CA: University of California, Regents.

Judicious Discipline from a Neurological Perspective:
Providing Context for Living and Learning in Our Democratic Society
—By Paul Gathercoal—

Specific strategies for school discipline and classroom management that are based on models of behavior modification have become increasingly popular in American schools (Hill, 1990). As a result, most of our teachers and administrators have learned to mete out rewards and punishment in a systematic and *ad-hoc* fashion in hopes of controlling America's youth by reinforcing desirable behavior and discouraging unwanted behavior (McEwan, 1990). For many students, punishment or behaving out of fear of "getting caught" is the only model of discipline they experience throughout their formal schooling. And models of discipline that are based on fear and coercion operate only at the lowest levels of ethical reasoning on any taxonomy of moral development.

It is not surprising, then, that the reaction from America's youth to these behavioral models of discipline has not been favorable. When asked, students who attended schools where behavioral models of discipline were in force often tell me that they and their classmates felt "powerless." Possibly it is this feeling of powerlessness that has contributed to the large number of students "at risk" in American schools (Sarason, 1990). Behavioral models of school discipline have done little to instill a sense of responsible behavior in students and change is needed.

William Glasser (1985) echoes this call for change when he says educators must "give up" coercion and stimulus/response techniques in schools. He states there are only five genetically-determined intrinsic motivators or "basic needs" that will sustain the potential for teaching and learning: survival, freedom, love and belonging, power, and fun. These "basic needs" are the epistemological "heart and soul" of cognitive models for school discipline.

When educators decide to change school discipline and classroom management practices from a behavioral model to a cognitive model, the change must be implemented incrementally (Gathercoal, 1991). These things take time, because there is no context for understanding or visualizing cognitive discipline practices when the only model students, teachers, and parent(s)/caregiver(s) have known is coercive.

To exemplify this notion, I am reminded of one of my second-grade students who wrote and submitted an article to me for final editing and inclusion in our first class newsletter that was to be sent home to parent(s)/caregiver(s). In the article, the student expressed concern that there was a lot of fighting going on in our classroom and that I was doing nothing about it. It was early in the year, after we had addressed the principles of *Judicious Discipline* and established our class rules, but had yet to talk about consequences. As a result, my way of dealing with the behavior problems in the classroom was seen, at least by this student, as doing nothing about it. This was probably because the strategies I used were transparent to students who were not involved. This particular student saw no names on the board, heard no warnings being issued, and observed no public ridicule being meted out. There were, however, quiet talks that resulted in negotiated and commensurate consequences assigned to the offending behavior. All of this remained confidential, and so was not obvious to others until we talked about appropriate consequences as a class. It was quite some time later that the concerned student approached me and requested that I not publish the article "about the fighting in our class." Incremental changes based on present practice and extending toward future practice helped to provide context for change and make the new disciplinary practices apparent instead of transparent.

In order to help students and ourselves prepare for dramatic change, we must construct a framework for this process. We can do this by understanding that it takes time to educate our community of students, fellow educators, and parent/caregiver(s), while providing them with understandable metaphors for change (Langer, 1989; Lipsitt, 1990; Restak, 1988; Squire, 1987). These metaphors connect the new ideas embedded in *Judicious Discipline* to what are currently accepted practices.

Time is necessary because the fabric or context for change cannot be constructed overnight. In order to implement dramatic change, students, teachers and administrators, as well as parent(s)/caregiver(s), need **time** to **physically** construct new neurological connections in their brains (Edleman, 1987; Grossberg, 1980; Ornstein & Thompson, 1984). Incremental implementation of *Judicious Discipline*, which metaphorically links the new to the old, will help weave this fabric of neurological change. To better understand this need for **time**, **incremental implementation**, and **neuronal adaptation in the brain**, let us consider the biological link between cognition (thought) and behavior (action).

All Learning is Biological

Consider that the brain's shape and biochemical makeup is physically affected by an individual's experience and metaphorical imagination, and this affect is fueled by memory and perception (Kandel, Schwartz, & Jessell, 1991; Levinthal, 1990; Restak, 1988; Squire, 1987). In other words, the brain is "plastic." It is a combination of our experience and metaphorical imaginings that help to construct new neurological connections—a fabric for change. As a result, the brain continually adapts to new input and redefines appropriate behavior, and this is reflected in our ever-changing ideas, beliefs, attitudes, and values. We physically construct neuronal circuits with balanced states of biochemical and electrical activity and these become our conceptual maps of social reality and our cultural ways of knowing; these are our schemata.

This is how we learn and know how to behave. We change biologically and act accordingly (Kandel, *et. al.*, 1991; Levinthal, 1990; Ornstein & Thompson, 1984). Given this close association between experience and imagination, cognition and behavior, it is logical to think that if an individual only experiences coercive, stimulus/response classroom management practices, s/he will probably learn to operate at the lowest levels of moral development. S/he will constantly ask, "What's in it for me?" because that is the way s/he will be "wired" to respond. For students who have been subjected to coercive/behavioral models of school discipline for most of their lives, the proposition of being held accountable or responsible for their own learning and behavior can be a shock to their neuronal circuits. After years of fine tuning neuronal circuits which activate behavior designed to avoid possible punishment and seek probable rewards, it may be difficult for students to come to terms with the rigors of being self-disciplined, responsible citizens in a democratic classroom. Students will need to be taught about their democratic rights and responsibilities and given the **time** and opportunities to experience and imagine so they can **physically** change their neuronal connections and biochemical activity in order to accommodate the new experience of living and learning in a democratic environment.

Judicious Discipline provides educators with opportunities to challenge their students' neuronal circuits by offering students "neurological time" to consider alternatives. Imagine the opportunities for teaching and learning when students with problems are requested by the educator to "Tell me about it" instead of confronted with "Who dunit?" Rather than activating what is known as a stereotypical response circuit, i.e., "It wasn't me!," students are given an opportunity to take "neurological time" and access other ideas via alternative neuronal circuits. They enjoy an opportunity to tell the educator about their problem. In so doing, they access neuronal circuits that recall perceptions, offer explanations, make predictions, and suggest possible choices. These are the higher-level thinking processes that educators hope to tap into during every lesson. It follows that educators who practice *Judicious Discipline* will give their students repeated opportunities for practicing higher-level thinking. And as a result, it is likely that "It wasn't me!" will disappear from students' repertoire of stereotypical responses. Concomitantly, they will learn to favor more self-reflecting responses that indicate an ownership of behavior and a responsibility for their actions.

The Endorphin Connection

Endorphins (**End**ogenous **M**orphines) are very powerful peptides, composed of small chains of amino acids. They act as neurotransmitters (the basic unit of action in the brain). When released in the brain, they attach themselves to receptors on specific brain cells or neurons.

Endorphins are very important. Our bodies physically need them. In fact, we are addicted to endorphin activity. If we do not synthesize, release, and bind endorphins to specific brain cells we will go through a "withdrawal" similar to that of a heroin addict (Beck & Beck, 1987; Levinthal, 1988).

Endorphins are involved in maintaining health; mediating emotions, pain, and stress; and providing intrinsic reward (Kehoe, 1988). They perform these functions by relieving pain and/or inducing feelings of pleasure. It is the endorphin link with intrinsic reward that is most fascinating and adds support to Glasser's (1985) notion that there are five genetically determined intrinsic motivators. In fact, all five of Glasser's "basic needs" can be genetically explained, at least in part, as being mediated by endorphin activity in the brain.

Consider that individuals can be predisposed to certain behaviors that are mediated by endorphin activity; that is, an individual may get a "good feeling" because s/he acts a certain way in a social situation. Inappropriate behaviors in school, when interpreted in this light, can then be viewed as behaviors that are endorphin activating for one student but infringing on the rights and interests of the rest of the class. Teachers responding to such inappropriate behavior with coercive, stimulus/response discipline strategies probably believe they can provide students with extrinsic rewards that will exceed the intrinsic rewards of endorphin activity students probably feel when they display the inappropriate behavior.

The problem with this approach is that the offending behavior still acts as endorphin-activating experiences, and the student has acquired new ways of seeking "love and belonging," "power," "freedom," "fun," and even "survival" that are all dependent upon the school providing tangible reinforcers. In other words, the student never owns the problem, but reaps even more benefits as a result of it and always at the expense of others. The student who is put on a behavior modification program to control "attention getting" outbursts in class is still in a power struggle with authority. S/he is still intent upon seeking power through acquiring some form of tangible reward—whether it be positive comments from the teacher or "beans-in-a-jar"—and if the rewards for conforming to the teacher's expectations are not great enough, s/he need only resort to the offensive behavior once more to assert power over the class environment.

Only when the desired behavior is intrinsically rewarding to the student will s/he ultimately change. *Judicious Discipline* can assist with this transition by helping misbehaving students imagine ways they can meet their "physical needs" for socially stimulated endorphin activity by behaving in institutionally okay ways and helping to provide a neurological context for change at the same time.

The Effect of Media Messages on Behavior

Another effect of endorphin activity may be closely linked to modeling via the media and their messages. Students who continually rely on commercial media messages for role models and use them as guides for mentally rehearsing successful social behaviors are probably glorifying behaviors that are antithetical to acceptable, ethical behavior in schools. Students who emulate their favorite star's mannerisms and stereotyped behaviors may expect violence and coercion to solve problems, think that any social problem can be completely solved within a short period of time, and that sex role stereotypes are accurate reflections of our society and the expected norm. Consider the majority of "007" films screened in cinemas around the world, re-run on commercial television, and rented on videotape. Male students may learn from the featured male role model that to be successful in love they need to act macho and aloof, and treat women as mere objects. Female students may learn that they need to be slender, with "perfect" hair and teeth, and that they **are** mere objects for men's pleasure. While educators try very hard to instill a sense of "it's okay to be you and me," the messages of the commercial media tend to compromise this premise in a very powerful way. And even these students with the strongest self-concept will pause a moment to compare their self-images with those images presented by the commercial media.

Judicious Discipline helps combat these messages by offering a framework for discussing the dichotomy of values and popular messages while providing a student-centered approach to school discipline and classroom management that gives students a sense of "permanent value" (Dreikurs, 1968). Teaching students about individual rights and responsibilities conveys the message that everyone has a right to feel physically and mentally safe and secure and that everyone has a responsibility to ensure that these feelings extended throughout society. Students learn that they are important individuals, too, especially when the judicious educator takes time to listen to their side of the story, acts with professional courage, and negotiates appropriate consequences for breaches in rules. Implicitly, the educator is sending a powerful message about the importance of the individual.

This kind of behavior from educators is antithetical to the behavior generally displayed in commercial films and television. When modeling such alternative behaviors for students, the judicious educator is laying a context, a fabric of neurological connections, that helps prepare students for ideological change. Educators who model behavior based on democratic principles implicitly challenge their students to question the fantastic nature of superhero behaviors and the "glitz" associated with dramatized films and commercial television programs.

Providing Context: A Role for *Judicious Discipline*

Individuals who need greater and greater endorphin activity to achieve a "good feeling," or who constantly activate specific, stereotypical neuronal circuitry in response to social and problem situations, may become caught up in their own pleasure and be desensitized to the needs and desires of their living environment. This is where *Judicious Discipline* can provide a new context for understanding and assist individuals to realize that their rights are always balanced against the interests of the rest of society. Through education (involving experience and metaphorical imagination) we can affect student cognition and behavior by helping them make new neuronal connections.

The effect of implementing *Judicious Discipline* will be to construct a cerebral context for critical thinking. But the reality is that this effect will not be immediate; it will take **time**.

However, the good news is that the effect will probably be long lasting and transferable from one situation to another. Educators need to realize that **time** is an educational resource that we have available to us and we should expand time to accommodate and tap into the "basic needs" of our students (fun, power, freedom, love and belonging, and survival).

As educators we should realize that we affect our students by physically changing their genetic makeup, through experience and metaphorical imagination, that affects their predisposition for cognition and behavior. Only cognitive models for school discipline, like *Judicious Discipline*, will effect such long-lasting change in our students. Coercive, stimulus/response models will only effect change for specific situations; and unless accompanied by some intrinsic motivation, the learned behavior will not be transferred from problem situation to problem situation. It is cognitive models, like *Judicious Discipline*, that will help prepare our nation's students for living and learning in a democratic society.

References & Sources

Bachevalier, J. (1990). Ontogenetic development of habit and memory formation in primates. In A. Diamond (Ed.) *The development and neural bases of higher cognitive functions.* New York: The New York Academy of Sciences.

Beck, D., & Beck, J. (1987). *The pleasure connection.* San Francisco, CA: Synthesis Press.

DeFleur, M.L., & Ball-Rokeach, S. (1990). *Theories of mass communication*, 5th Ed., White Plains, NY: Longman.

Dreikurs, R. (1968). *Psychology in the classroom: A manual for teachers*, 2nd Ed. New York: Harper & Row.

Edleman, G.M. (1987). *Neural darwinism: The theory of neuronal group selection.* New York: Basic Books.

Gardner, L.R. (1983). *Frames of mind: The theory of multiple intelligences.* New York: Basic Books.

Gathercoal, F. (1993, 3rd edition). *Judicious discipline.* San Francisco, CA: Caddo Gap Press.

Gathercoal, P. (1990). Brain research and mediated experience: An interpretation of the implications for education. *The Clearing House*, 63(6), 271-273.

Gathercoal, P. (1991). A technology for policy implementation: Minimizing incongruity between ostensible policy and the policy at work. *Educational Technology*, 31(3), 47-50.

Glasser, W. (1986). *Control theory in the classroom.* New York: Harper & Row.

Goldstein, A. (1980). Thrills in response to music and other stimuli. *Physiological Psychology*, 8(1), 126-129.

Grossberg, S. (1980). How does a brain build a cognitive code? *Physiological Review*, 87(1), 1-39.

Hill, D. (April, 1990). Order in the classroom. *Teacher.* 70-77.

Kandel, E.R., Schwartz, J.H., & Jessell, T. M. (1991). *Principles of neural science*, 3rd Ed. New York: Elsevier.

Kehoe, P. (1988). Opiods, behavior, and learning in mammalian development. In E.M. Blass (Ed.) *Handbook of behavioral neurobiology: Volume 9: Developmental psychobiology and behavioral ecology.* (pp. 309-346). New York: Plenum Press.

Lammers, J.H.C.M., van der Noordaa, J., Kruk, M.R., Meelis, W., & van der Poel, G.M. (1989). Interactions between simultaneously activated behavioral systems in the rat. *Behavioral Neuroscience*, 103(4), 784-789.

Langer, E.J. (1989). *Mindfulness.* Reading, MA: Addison-Wesley.

Levinthal, C.F. (1990). *Introduction to physiological psychology.* Englewood Cliffs, NJ: Prentice Hall.

Levinthal, C.F. (1988). *Messengers of paradise: Opiates and the brain.* New York: Anchor Press.

Levitt, R.A., Stilwell, D.J., & Evers, T.M. (1978). Brief communication: Morphine and shuttle-box self-stimulation in the rat: Tolerance studies. *Pharmacology Biochemistry & Behavior*, 9, 567-569.

Lipsitt, L.P. (1990). Learning processes in the human newborn. In A. Diamond (Ed.) *The development and neural bases of higher cognitive functions.* New York: The New York Academy of Sciences.

McEwan, B. (1990). Review: Judicious discipline. *Democracy and Education*, 4(3), 37-40.

Ornstein, R., & Ehrlich, P. (1990). *New world new mind.* New York: Simon & Schuster.

Ornstein, R., & Thompson, R.F. (1984). *The amazing brain.* Boston: Houghton Mifflin.

Restak, R.M. (July/August, 1992). See no evil: The neurological defense would blame violence on the damaged brain. *The Sciences*. 16-21.

Restak, R.M. (1988). *The mind*. New York: Bantam Books.

Sarason, S.B. (1990). *The predictable failure of educational reform*. San Francisco, CA: Jossey-Bass Publishers.

South Australian Council for Children's Films and Television, Inc. (1986). *Kids and the scary world of video*. A Study of Video Viewing Among 1498 Primary School Children in South Australia, published by the Television Committee of the South Australian Council for Children's Films and Television, Inc.

Squire, L.R. (1987). *Memory and brain*. New York: Oxford University Press.

Visual Learners:

Creating Equity in the Classroom for Diverse Learning Styles
—By Charlene DeLage—

After spending a great deal of time in school creating pictures in my head, I have come to realize that those ideas and concepts that held the most meaning for me always carried some sort of visual image. When I was exposed to visual or auditory information, I would remember it by linking it to pictures I'd visually created. If I wasn't mentally creating images, I'd be graphically recording them by either trying to make an accurate illustration of an idea or just some doodles on my notepaper. Many times this method of perceiving information was very satisfactory, whereas at other times I was not learning the information, but only remembering my images.

Now, as a teacher, I look back on my experiences in school and I wonder how other children might be perceiving their reality in terms of the educational opportunities they are being offered. My own interest in addressing the learning capacities of students comes in part from my own experience as well as an investigation into other writings and research. The book *Unicorns are Real* (Vitale, 1982) expresses ideas about learning styles that clearly explain differences among student abilities. In her book, Barbara M. Vitale writes "each child is the center of his own universe." Children see their world as it relates to their own inner understandings before they are able to comprehend the interpretations of others. In addition to Vitale's ideas, I have also become aware of work by Rudolph Arnheim (1977) concerning studies of the intellectual and intuitive growth of children and how that growth relates to individual capacities for constructing knowledge. With the construction of this knowledge, David Olson (1977) has pursued the investigation into avenues of expression through symbolization other than linguistic or mathematical symbols our culture teaches.

The movement to study how children learn has spawned several investigations. The research of Howard Gardner in the area of Multiple Intelligences addresses the complexity of how children's biological makeup and early experiences have an effect on the development of individual capacities. My interest in visual-spatial abilities and visual construction of knowledge relates to Gardner's ideas of the seven intelligences theory, particularly to the category of spatial intelligence. This category is described as encompassing the capacity of an individual "to perceive the visual world accurately, to perform transformations and modifications upon one's initial perceptions, and to be able to re-create aspects of one's visual experience, even in the absence of relevant physical stimuli" (Gardner, 1983) Students like myself, who reach first for the picture, need to have that picture linked to the auditory information presented. Whether pictures of new information are created randomly in the heads of students, are drawn by students, or are visually presented by the teacher, each image plays an important role in the learning process.

To practice *Judicious Discipline* is to find ways of reaching all students by meeting their educational needs. To ensure equal educational opportunity for visual learners, I begin by making sure I always support verbal information with graphic illustrations recorded on a flip chart, overhead transparency, blackboard, or another suitable medium. As a teacher, I now can look back on my own learning, synthesize my readings into research on learning styles, and draw conclusions about how best to teach visual learners in my own classroom. I know that the drawings do not have to be beautiful or perfect, they just have to be there. It is important though to avoid cluttering the illustration with unnecessary information— erase or cover up any extraneous words or pictures that are near your immediate focal point. As students get older this may not be as much of a problem, but it depends on what it is you want them to be aware of and your best judgment about how much unnecessary, visually-confusing information it takes to interfere with a concept that otherwise would be clearly conveyed. Even older students could benefit from boxing out peripheral information that isn't key to your current lesson.

The classroom environment has a significant effect on the way students perform. If they are distracted by the arrangement of the furniture or too much graphic stimulation, it becomes difficult for visual learners to focus. My visual antennae are always out and it takes a minimum of stimulation for me to be distracted. I know that when I want to focus the attention of my visual learners on specific areas, I need to leave nearby areas free from conflicting visual "stuff." If I notice that students are confused by my directions about the room, I look again at how I have created the space for them. Organizing central areas for papers, books, projects, etc. will help them be less confused and more accountable for the shared educational experience in my classroom.

Tests and handouts can also be visually confusing. It is important to look at the pages of a handout to see how much visual information you are including on each and how closely the directions match the layout of the items. In other words, if you ask a question designed to be answered with a brief essay, but only allow a small space for the answer, visual learners may not be able to sort out the confusion created. I have noticed that standardized tests have pages that are over-packed with questions and do not seem to take into account how one page relates to another. When I develop a test, I make sure that if one page is busy with a large amount of information or questions, then I alter the layout on the next page. I want to give my students a chance to rest their eyes and not tune out or become tired from the appearance of too many expectations.

The current trend in children's literature (Short, 1993) focuses on the use of visual literacy as a help in understanding a book's content. The prevalence and high quality of illustrations appearing in children's books motivate visual learners to actively engage in the reading process. "Writer's Workshop" is a classroom method of teaching writing to students that directly ties visual images with the printed word. As young students draw, then write about their illustrations, they begin to develop increased skills in both areas. Any time a teacher can help students link the use of visuals with learning experiences, they provide an opportunity for greater comprehension. When presenting this opportunity to students, teachers need to be aware of the materials provided for rough draft copies and how they relate to what will be used for the final draft. Crayons, markers, water colors, or other marking medium should be the same for all copies. Because visual learners will have a mental image of how each draft should look, it is important that the type of paper used should also be the same. Using paper that is horizontal for the draft and vertical for the final copy can be a very difficult problem for students who have planned illustrations to fit a specific area.

While exploring ways to provide visual learners with exciting opportunities, teachers should consider how technology will fit this goal. Although I have not researched all the aspects of educational software, providing visual learners with an opportunity to work on computers opens the door for many exciting possibilities. It has the potential of being the tool that provides them with flexible learning experiences. In order to derive maximum use from computer programs, read about them and try them out before introducing them.

Finally, being aware of how to present information is important in all aspects of teaching. Expanding current teaching practices to include the integration of different ways of knowing helps to ensure that all learners will be invited into the educational process. Bruce Campbell of New Horizons for Learning has used a unique method for implementing a curriculum based on the seven intelligences. Here is a graphic illustrating his method of instruction:

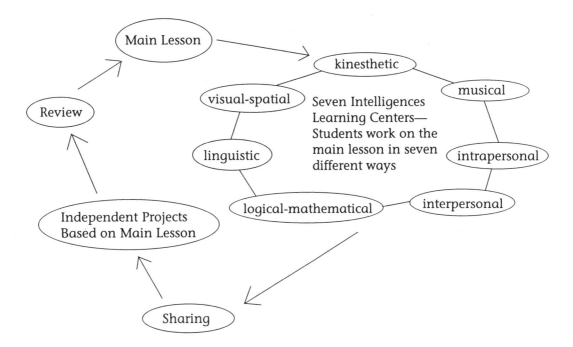

   As the graphic illustrates, students all begin the day by discussing the main lesson or idea the instructor wants to teach. Then students break off into one of the seven learning groups. This same lesson is then addressed in seven different ways. After each student experiences each group, the class comes together to share how they have approached the lesson. Later, students have the opportunity to work on the information again, this time focusing on their own learning mode, allowing them to exercise their own talents and abilities while developing a more indepth understanding of what is being taught. Finally, students come together again to debrief and review. This approach to teaching not only encourages strengths but also allows for students to experience learning in their weaker areas as well. If deficiencies are not equally encouraged, students will be less apt to develop balanced ways of approaching problems. Working with both the strengths and weaknesses of students provides teachers with not only meaningful assessment information, but also the understanding of how to improve future curriculum designs.
   Student self-esteem is complemented and enhanced through the deliberate decisions made by their teachers. Teachers wanting to avoid the experience of trying to work with students who are disinterested and exhibiting inappropriate behaviors must make the effort to ensure equal educational opportunities through curriculum design. Understanding how to effectively address the needs of students with varying learning styles can only improve their chances to achieve and excel.

References

Arhheim, Rudolf, "The Double-Edged Mind: Intuition and the Intellect", *Learning and Teaching the Ways of Knowing*, ed. Elliot Eisner, 1985

Campbell, Bruce, Linda Campbell, & Dee Dickinson, *Teaching and Learning Through Multiple Intelligences*, New Horizons for Learning, Seattle, 1992.

Gardner, Howard, *Frames of Mind*, Basic Books, New York, 1983

Olson, David R., "The Arts as Basic Skills: Three Cognitive Functions of Symbols," *The Arts, Cognition, and Basic Skills*, CEMREL, Inc., St. Louis, 1977

Short, Kathy G., "Visual Literacy: Exploring Art and Illustration in Children's Books," *The Reading Teacher*, 1993

Vitale, Barbara, M., *Unicorns Are Real*, Warner Books, New York, 1982

Educators Talk about Judicious Discipline

My Experience
—By Bill Lee—

I was not in the market for a "new" classroom management program when I was introduced to *Judicious Discipline* in the Fall of 1988. The one I was using, although quite stressful for me, seemed to work well enough. And it was based on some pretty solid and historical traits—intimidation, coercion, and threats. I set the rules—the students followed them, or else. So when a colleague at Cortland College asked me to read Forrest Gathercoal's *Judicious Discipline* to see if it was something I could use, I reluctantly agreed.

Leafing through the book, my first impressions were—"Too theoretical. Too technical. Too much legalese." But before I returned the book to my friend with my negative reaction, I began to read the Preface. Two sentences later, Gathercoal had captured my attention. There in print was "my philosophy" of classroom management and student behavior. The wording was a bit different, but the message was the same: "You may do what you want in this classroom until it interferes with the rights of the other students." I read on.

The foundation of *Judicious Discipline* was the rights provided by the United States Constitution and the responsibilities of the four "Compelling State Interests," basically the guidelines that allow us all to live together in a relatively safe and sane environment. Their effect in the classroom was to put the onus of behavior on the students and not on the teacher. Yes, students did have rights, and those rights should be protected. But those same students bear responsibility for their actions so as to not infringe upon the rights of others. It seemed to reflect the same belief I held but had had trouble instilling in my students. It was not enough to say when questioned about a rule, "Do it because I said so." That put the burden of student behavior on me. But with the concepts of *Judicious Discipline*, there was a framework and a justification for why students should conduct themselves in a manner which would not be detrimental to themselves or their fellow classmates.

I wanted to try this *Judicious Discipline* thing, but I needed more information and support. I obtained both from Barbara McEwan, as Assistant Professor of Education at Cortland College. She had worked with Gathercoal on the development of the model and was conducting research on its applications. She provided me with lesson plans used in a school in Oregon and gave me some guidance. I implemented the model the first day of the second semester.

"This is Social Studies. Why are we doing Social Studies in English class?" My students were as receptive as I had been before I read the Preface of *Judicious Discipline*. I pressed on. The rights under the United States Constitution came first. Then the four "Compelling State Interests" and the balance between the two. Using situational role playing and case studies of students' challenges to school rules, my eighth graders were able to identify the constitutional rights and "Compelling State Interests." Further, they discovered and came to appreciate the difficult time the legal system has balancing the rights of the individual with those of the group. They went through the rules and regulations found in the school's student handbook and labeled each with the "Compelling State Interest" used to create it. They were beginning to take a more informed view of classroom management and behavior.

The next step was to develop classroom rules. I use a lot of cooperative and group learning in my classes, so I had groups begin to write a set of classroom rules. They wrote too many rules that were too specific—"No gum chewing," "No leaning back in your chair," etc. I had them refocus on the "Compelling State Interests." Before long, each group produced four broad classroom rules based on the needs of society. While their rules were still written from a negative perspective, they were now putting the onus for behavior on themselves. A committee from each of my classes rewrote them in a positive mode and adopted them as the classroom rules.

Since the students had written the rules and knew the justification for them, they were followed. I am not trying to deceive you—things were not perfect—but I am saying the classroom environment improved. Students began to take responsibility for their actions. I noticed a marked improvement in completion of assignments, especially homework assignments. The classroom became the students' and not just "Mr. Lee's room." They kept it cleaner than before, even "policing" those who weren't so neat. The incidents of horseplay and damage to furniture went way down. Finally, the students were taking responsibility for themselves and not relying on me to "nag" them in to proper classroom behavior.

There are still bugs. I need to do a better job with consequences and keeping my distance, allowing students an opportunity to take control of their own behavior. But, overall, *Judicious Discipline* works.

Judicious Discipline and Grading Practices
—By Daniel Blaufus—

The most immediate outcome from my participation in the course titled "The Law of Public Education" taught by Forrest Gathercoal and my reading of his *Judicious Discipline* book is reflected in my classroom management style. The entire atmosphere of my class and the relationship I have with my students has been radically changed. My old emphasis on discipline and deadlines has been replaced with compassion, understanding, and the best interest of the individual. It's remarkable to me how much I am suddenly enjoying teaching and how much my students are finding me to be an adult to whom they can turn for understanding. There have been times in my years of teaching when individuals have known that I genuinely care about them, but with a few alterations in my approach, I now have 125 students who feel I am really working for them.

These changes have come about through implementing many of the strategies outlined in *Judicious Discipline*. I feel very comfortable emphasizing to parents and students that the course work is important and must be completed. When parents come in for explanations of their child's Incomplete, my remarks make sense and show profound respect for the student and the subject matter. Every encounter I have had with parents and students has been very positive, because the choice is left with them. Not all students have made up the Incompletes, and, when the counseling department comes to me to find out what grade the child earned, I give them my best professional assessment of the student's knowledge. I finally feel like a professional educator and not a youth-group leader trying to instill all sorts of values and behaviors before I can give a grade.

Changing Attitudes and Practices

—By Rick Knode—

Judicious Discipline! I first heard of this concept from Margaret Abbott, a fellow student in one of my administration classes at Lewis and Clark College. When I heard her discuss the fact that students in a classroom have rights protected by the United States Constitution, the Oregon Constitution, and our judiciary system, I was stunned. I have been teaching for eighteen years and, during this entire time, I never once considered the notion that students have rights. I was, and to some extent still am, controlled by the oft heard saying of the teaching profession, "When those kids come through the door to my class, they have no rights except the ones I give them." However, I am working hard to change that belief through new methods of teaching. I am eventually hoping to carry the change over into my new role of school administrator.

I would like to review my classroom management style and reflect on ways *Judicious Discipline* has had an effect upon the decisions I make. Most times when I am conducting class, I have a cup of coffee at my side. I have given myself the right to drink in front of my students but will not allow them the same right. Also there have been times when I would eat something a student or fellow teacher would bring me, but forbid my students to eat. When students asked me why, I said: "This is my classroom! You will do what I say. If you do not like it, there is the door. It opens both ways!" I felt as if I never had to explain any decision I made. Although this may seem tyrannical, it seemed to me to be an appropriate management style.

I have quietly revised the rules in my classroom in regards to eating. When students do bring something for nourishment, I say nothing to them. With a wink of my eye or by establishing proximity, I do give notice to the fact that they are eating. However, if it is not disruptive to the educational process, I let it go. It is amazing what effect this insignificant change has had in my classroom. My stress level has been reduced and the students seem much happier.

Another classroom rule I had was related to bringing books, pencils, and papers to class in order to participate in the daily activities. Following our school's "Assertive Discipline" policy, if students were not prepared for class, they would receive detention. Once students accumulated three detentions, they would be given two or three days of in-school suspension. The next step would be out-of-school detention leading to expulsion. All of this for not bringing materials to class. The question is not "Does the punishment fit the crime?" but "Is this a crime at all?"

I now take a different approach to the issue of coming prepared to class. I keep several books on hand in the classroom for individuals who have left them at home or mistakenly taken the wrong book out of their lockers. I keep a supply of paper handy for those who do not have their own and I provide pencils, as well. This seems a much more reasonable solution than receiving detention for something over which students often have no control.

Finally, I have, in the past, forbidden boys to wear hats in the classroom. I felt this rule was sensible because well-bred individuals would not wear hats inside. I never asked students why they wore hats, I would just say "Take it off." There was never a chance of appeal and there were no exceptions to this rule.

At the start of this school year, I had a student who was going through treatment for cancer. Consequently, he had lost most of his hair and liked to wear a hat. I made an exception to my rule for him, and, as a result, other students pressed me to let them keep their hats on also. I agreed to do this only as long as "Jim" would need to wear his hat. Well, "Jim" no longer needs his hat, he passed away. I have ceased to make hats an issue in my class. The experience was a tough lesson for me on individual rights.

I know that I do not have the answers to every discipline problem that may occur. But, I hope that by allowing students to have the opportunity to engage in a learning process that develops from the balance of student rights and responsibilities, they will become better citizens and the school environment will improve.

Using *Judicious Discipline* as a Springboard to the Community
—By Betty Powers—

At the time of my introduction to *Judicious Discipline* I had been teaching long enough to feel comfortable with my classroom management system. I was really in for a shock when I enrolled in "Law and the Public School Teacher" taught by Barbara McEwan. Many practices that I thought were working well I now discovered should not have even been in my classroom at all. So I set about changing my policies and making the class a more judicious one. There were some basic changes I started with—I became more democratic and flexible in my approach to student problems. Instead of acting as the "rule giver" and enforcer, I became a facilitator and negotiator. I found myself in the position of being a student advocate rather than a top-down manager. Teaching in our newly-developed community was more enjoyable than it had been for years.

In the beginning, I sometimes found myself questioning my adherence to a system that was not always in the mainstream of popularity; especially, I implemented alternative activities in place of more traditional religious holiday celebrations. While many around me decorated bulletin boards, scheduled activities, and put on parties that contained religious overtones, my classroom seemed noticeably devoid of certain common symbols. Some parents questioned me about my policies. My students, however, always explained it to them. The students understood that respect for all views within a school was more important than celebrating one particular religious perspective.

I also had to work through this change with my professional colleagues. One conversation powerfully reinforced for me the decision I had made concerning this issue. I was discussing an upcoming holiday with a fellow teacher, and I commented that she didn't have her decoration up yet. This was a teacher who always took time to elaborately decorate her room for each holiday. Her response to me was "Oh, this isn't my holiday, so I don't put anything up." At that moment, I had a clear understanding of how teachers can inadvertently support one religion over another, and why the framers of the Constitution felt it was important that all people should feel free to practice their own beliefs apart from the school or state. Religious activities and bulletin boards have been replaced in my classroom with celebrations of the seasons and content-related materials that all students can enjoy.

In addition to establishing an overall positive climate, I saw other outgrowths of *Judicious Discipline*. Our students began to develop into more responsible citizens in the classroom and in their community. In order to further encourage this growth, I organized a service club for students in my school that would provide opportunities to become more actively involved in our town. We have averaged sixty participating students for each of the past three years. Their projects have all had a focus of reaching out to others. It has been one of the most rewarding experiences I have had in teaching. I have also found opportunities for my students to work on an intergenerational project. The result of this undertaking has been a greater understanding between senior citizens and fourth graders. As the concepts of *Judicious Discipline* have blossomed, the world has become our classroom and my students its citizens.

Part Two

Judicious Discipline Lesson Plans

Introduction
to Part Two

Part Two of this volume represents the work of many educators from all levels and disciplines. They have graciously submitted lesson plans that they have used or designed for use in their classes to introduce the concepts of *Judicious Discipline*—rights, compelling state interests, due process, ethics, and other related topics.

The plans begin with introductory lessons and move on to activities that might best be presented a little later in the year. In addition, the plans have been ordered so that activities appropriate for primary levels appear first, with middle and secondary materials coming later in this section. Please remember that these lessons are only suggestions. We encourage you to use our ideas as springboards for your own creativity; and we sincerely hope that you will eventually share your ideas with us.

Tips on How To Use Judicious Discipline in Your Classroom Monday Morning

—By Barbara McEwan & Margaret Abbott—

1. Prepare a lesson plan or plans that will help you **introduce to students** the concept of the balance between individual rights and Compelling State Interests. If you are introducing these ideas in the middle of the year, point out to students how the existing classroom rules you have been using are already aligned with the Compelling State Interests, or how they might easily be reworked to reflect those interests. If you are implementing *Judicious Discipline* at the beginning of the year, use one of the lesson plans in this section of the book, or create one of your own.

2. As you guide your students through the process of creating **classroom rules**, make sure they are rules with which you can feel comfortable. A rule prohibiting eating or drinking in the classroom won't work for you if you are accustomed to sipping coffee while you teach. Similarly, if you are a teacher who pats students on the shoulder as a congratulatory gesture, a rule stating "Keep hands and feet to yourself" may place you in a position of contradicting your own rules.

3. Prepare a **letter to send home** to parents that will explain the new policies in your classroom and your rationale for using *Judicious Discipline* as a decision-making framework.

4. Design a poster that will inform students of your **professional ethics**. Consider it the equivalent of your personal *Hippocratic Oath*. Discuss your ethical beliefs briefly with your students, and then ask them to develop a set of classroom ethics. Post their statement of ethics next to your own.

5. Keep a basket of **in-class assignments**. If your students are absent, tell them that the work they missed can be found in the designated baskets.

6. Let students know that they will receive an Incomplete until their work is handed in. Explain that they will not be graded work down if an assignment is late, nor will you assign an "F" to it if it is not handed in. State clearly that **each assignment** has a Legitimate Educational Purpose and must be completed. Let them know you are there to help them achieve that goal.

7. Set up a system of **two baskets** in your classroom, one for late papers and one for papers in on time.Explain to your students that the papers in on time will be graded promptly and returned, but the papers that are in the late basket will be graded when you have time. Papers in the late basket may result in the student receiving an Incomplete.

8. If you need to speak with a student about a problem, whisper to the student, find a quiet corner, or step into the hallway so that your conversation can preserve the **confidentiality** to which the student is entitled.

9. Institute a policy of **alternative learning assignments** for students who are guilty of cheating. Let the students know that mastery of the information is the overriding issue and that another opportunity to demonstrate that mastery will be provided.

10. Model respect for the property of others by giving receipts to students when you must confiscate toys or other items that are creating a disruption. Let students know that the items will be returned to them at the end of the day when they bring you the receipts.

11. Teach students to chew gum and pass notes **responsibly** by using the guidelines of appropriate time, place, and manner. Engage students in a discussion of when and how note passing and gum chewing would not violate any of the compelling state interest parameters.

12. Understand that **you are the model** in your classroom for trust and tolerance. Your students watch you and take their cues from your actions. As situations occur, ask yourself "What needs to be learned here? What would an educator do?"

Establishing Judicious Discipline in the Primary Classroom
—By Margaret Abbott—

Teaching Rights and Responsibilities

Age group:
K-3.

Objective:
To encourage students in determining why rules are important. To help students understand that there are reasons for the rules that will guide classroom decisions during the year.

Time:
First of two thirty minute sessions.

Materials:
Crayons, paper, scissors, glue, large piece of butcher paper (cut to fit a bulletin board). An illustration of a scale and an actual scale.

Procedure:
Begin by having the students make a small paper model of themselves. Have each student place their paper model on the actual scale. Ask one student to move his/her model from the scale pan with all the other models in it to the side with none. Ask students to think of ways they could have the scales balance. Suggest to them that everyday they enter school they are in an imaginary scale with the teacher balancing their individual rights with the needs of all students. Explain that the rights of each student and the needs of all students are difficult to balance without rules.

Ask students what their rights are. Discuss with them the rights they will have some knowledge of, such as speech and expression. Be aware that children will often suggest rights they believe come to them from the Constitution, but in fact do not. (An example of this would be the right to a free, public education.) With third-graders, more time should be spent developing this distinction.

Go on to discuss what responsibilities they have in the classroom. Use a few examples to illustrate the concept of the scale. For instance, ask students if they think it would disturb their classroom if someone walked to the pencil sharpener. Then ask if there would be a problem if someone ran. Tip the scales on the individual side for walking, and on the other side for running. Running would be a violation of health and safety in the classroom and an individual student does not have the right to threaten the safety of others. It is the responsibility of each individual to move carefully for the good of everyone.

After a few of these examples, leave the scale as an example for the students to consider.

Review the rights that students have in the class and have children select to represent one of those rights with a drawing. Clearly explain that each child in the classroom has rights and that the single paper model on one side of the scale represents them. Glue the pictures on one side of the butcher paper.

End of first session.

Teaching the Compelling State Interests

Age group:
K-3.

Objective:
To help students understand their responsibilities in the classroom. To encourage students to help create classroom rules based on the Compelling State Interests.

Time:
Thirty minutes again.

Materials:
Same as before.

Procedure:
Help students recall Lesson #1 in this series. Ask students: "Why do we need rules?" "What kind of rules do we need?" "What rules would help our classroom to run smoothly and be a comfortable place for you?" "Do we need rules to help us stay safe?" "Should we have rules that protect our property, our stuff'?" "Would it help us to learn better if we had a rule about why we are in school?" "Do we need a rule to keep students from disrupting our study and work time?"

(With younger children, it would be appropriate to develop one concept at a time. For instance, health and safety could be the topic for one discussion session, saving the other Compelling State Interests for subsequent days.)

After you have presented all four Compelling State Interests, have each student select one and draw two pictures. The first should be of someone breaking a Compelling State Interest and the second should be of someone respecting a Compelling State Interest. Before they begin drawing, brainstorm together some ideas for what a picture might look like that illustrated someone not being safe, or quiet, or respecting the property of others. Then discuss what a picture might look like of someone being careful, etc.

On the sheet of butcher paper mentioned earlier, write the word "Rights" over the first set of pictures. Display pictures of what should not be done in a classroom and title that section "Reason for Rules." Finally, put "Needs" over the pictures of how they would like the classroom to be.

Have students explain their drawings to you before posting them. (It is most important that you ask their permission 'before displaying any of their drawings. Ask for permission on a one-to-one basis.)

End of second session.

Teaching Ethics
—By Margaret Abbott—

Lesson 1—Responsible

Age Group:
Adaptable for 1st through 6th grade.

Objective:
To stimulate an awareness of individual responsibility for one student toward other students, learning, and the school environment.

Time:
These lessons can be divided into two thirty minute sessions for younger students or can be presented as one forty-five minute session for older students.

Materials:
A pre-made chart on chart paper, crayons, scissors, construction or drawing paper, butcher paper, felt pens.

Chart

Being Responsible Is:	Yes	No
Picking up after myself—	X	
Being on time—	X	

Procedure:
Have students look at the chart you have started. Ask them to think of ways they are responsible for themselves. If they are hesitant, ask them prompts such as: "Do you do chores at home?" "Do you have a special routine to get ready for bed?" "Do you have responsibilities before you come to school?"

Ask students to help you finish the chart. Begin by asking what students should take responsibility for at school and with other students. Add all responses to the chart. Have students use felt pens to make x's under the yes column for each idea they offer.

(If working with younger children, this should be the end of the first 30-minute session).

Session 2:
(If breaking lesson into two sessions for younger children; otherwise procedures below should be continuation of procedures above as part of a single lesson).

Procedure:
Review chart, read it out loud. Have students put an * by the ones that have to do with school as the list is read. Hand out drawing paper. Have students draw a pictures of themselves being responsible with others at school, or with their school work, or with school property. Then ask them to cut out their pictures and glue them to the large piece of butcher paper. Have students share what they drew.

Lesson 2—**Helpful**

Age Group:
Adaptable for 1st through 6th grade.

Objective:
To achieve a significant appreciation and acceptance of how being helpful can enhance the classroom environment for cooperative learning and *Judicious Discipline*.

Time:
45 minutes (including clean up).

Materials:
Poster paper, construction paper, glue, scissors, and crayons.

Procedure:
Begin by having the class web the word "helpful." Record their ideas on butcher paper. Next divide the class into groups of four. Assign the following jobs: Materials gatherer and clean up person; cutter; gluer; and drawer. Provide the materials listed above with sufficient amounts for each group.

Ask the groups to briefly discuss how they look and what they say when they are being helpful. Then, each group should make a poster to display what they decided a group would look and sound like. At the end, discuss with the group how they think being helpful in their small groups might help the whole class. Record their ideas on poster board. Display the group pictures along with the recorded comments on a bulletin board.

Teaching Cooperation:
The Need for Rules
—By Thom Thompson—

Age Group:
Intermediate.

Objective:
To help students understand the need for rules in a classroom.

Time:
Approximately 30 minutes.

Materials:
Chalk, chalkboard.

Procedure:
One the board the teacher puts the model of a gallows and blanks for any word. Announce that the class will be playing "Hangman." (Suggestion: use blanks for DEMOCRACY, since you will continue to use the word in future lessons.)

Select an a student assistant. The role of the assistant will be to write correctly-guessed letters on any available blank. Privately instruct your assistant that it is not necessary to place the correct letters in the correct spaces.

Tell the students you and the assistant will play against the class, and that it is important for the class to win. Explain that if they lose they may have something taken away from them. Have students guess letters. If the letter is correct, have the assistant put the letter on any space while you say "The letter is correct, put it anywhere." Even if letters are correct, draw in various pieces of the hanged figure. Draw in one, two, or three pieces at a time.

When the class loses, tell them that you will play them double or nothing in another game. Do not be specific about what will be lost.

Construct a tic-tac-toe model and give the class the first X placement. Have the assistant place an O and then you should place your own O. The class gets one more X and the two people at the board win on their next selections.

Students will, of course, be complaining that you are cheating.

Discussion:

First, inform the students they have not lost anything. Tell them that you were not cheating, nor were you being unfair, because you were playing by your own rules. You simply did not play by the rules with which they are familiar.

Ask students why it is better to know the rules and what to do if there is a disagreement on the rules.

Finish this discussion with: "I would like you to help me make the rules in this room. Tomorrow I will be explaining your constitutional rights and citizenship responsibilities. When you understand the framework for our classroom rules, you will be able to help me write four rules that will be fair and equitable."

Understanding Rights and Creating Rules in a Democratic Classroom

—By Barbara McEwan & Margaret Abbott—

Age Group:
4th-8th grade.

Objective:
To inform students of their rights and when they lose their rights according to society's needs. To provide students with an opportunity to apply that information to the development of classroom rules.

Time:
35 to 40 minutes.

Materials:
Butcher paper, markers, enough copies of the Constitution for five or six groups, and a poster listing the Compelling State Interests.

Procedure:
Begin by saying "Take out a piece of paper and pencil. As fast as you can, write down all the individual rights you think you have in our country. " Ask for their responses and record them on the chalkboard. Then say "Now, write down all the rights you think you have when you are in school." Put these responses on the board. Ask "Would you be surprised to find out that your rights as citizens of our country and your rights in school are almost the same?"

Continue by saying "Today we will be discussing the citizenship rights you have in a public school classroom and when you can lose those rights.

"Understanding the rights we all have and knowing what actions can cause us to lose those rights helps us to become responsible citizens in school and in our society.

"Let's look again at the rights we've put on the board. Let's see if there is a way to group them into categories. First, how do we know we have these rights? Who or what tells us that we do?"

Guide students through a brief review of the Constitution and Amendments.
"In school you have all your rights protected. You even have more rights in a classroom than I do." (Use example of students wearing political buttons. Point out why it is important

for teachers to refrain from such a statement.)

"Primarily there are three Amendments that are very important to remember in school: the First, Fourth, and Fourteenth." At this point, form the class into five or six groups and have them review those three amendments.

"Tell me which of the rights on the board would come from the First Amendment? The Fourth? The Fourteenth? Are there any rights left over that we haven't labeled? Look again at the Bill of Rights and see if you can find where those rights might fit? Are they really constitutional rights after all?

"You are citizens in my classroom and you know your rights. I will treat you as citizens and work very hard to protect your rights.

"I am a citizen in this town, state, and country. When I'm not in this classroom I am entitled to all of my rights. What does that mean? Does that mean I can do anything I want to? Can I do anything I feel like doing?"

Brainstorm and list on the board actions that any adult should refrain from doing as a citizen, such as running a stop sign or yelling "Fire" in a theater.

"When we put your rights on the board, we were able to group them under the heading of different Amendments. Let's look at your ideas about when I lose my rights and see if we can discover some headings those actions might fit under. In your groups, work together to see if you can discover headings or categories for the situations on the board."

In five minutes, check to see if they have discovered any patterns to the actions. Put their ideas for categories on the board and display a poster listing the Compelling State Interests. Briefly explain them.

"When society takes away my rights, they do it because of a Compelling State Interest. I can't throw a rock through a store window, or run a red light, or yell fire in a theater. As citizens in this classroom, you will lose your rights if I can show a Compelling State Interest applies to something you are doing. Let's look again at the Compelling State Interests. In your groups take a few minutes to discuss what actions students might engage in that would result in them losing their rights."

In five minutes, bring the groups back together to share their ideas.

"Now that you have an understanding of what rights you have and when you can lose those rights, let's begin to think of how we can develop classroom rules that reflect the Compelling State Interests. For instance, what do you think a workable rule might be based on Property Loss and Damage?"

In small groups, have them brainstorm class rules based on the needs of society. Have groups share their ideas. Wording should be very similar. Record each of the four rules, reaching consensus on the wording. The key to consensus should be the scope of the rule developed. For instance, encourage students to consider the broader applicability of a rule that says "Respect the property of others" as opposed to a rule stating "Don't write on desks." Help students to decide on rules that will cover all imaginable situations.

"Now that we have discussed your citizenship rights and developed rules base on the Compelling State Interests, we are ready for the next step. Tomorrow we will talk about judicious consequences. We will discuss what they are and how they will be applied."

Establishing Commensurate and Compatible Consequences

—By Margaret Abbott—

Age group:
4th-6th grade.

Objective:
To establish a set of consequences for behaviors that do not comply with class rules.

Time:
20 to 25 minutes.

Procedure:
Teacher says "We have discussed how we expect people to behave and we have created a set of rules to remind us of that discussion. But sometimes people will forget. When that happens, I will work with those people to remind them of our rules and help them understand why it is important to follow the rules. On occasion, it may be necessary for the people who broke a rule to experience a consequence that will help them remember the rule next time.

"Because I want to help you remember the rules and learn how to follow them, I will work hard to make sure that the consequence fits whatever rules have been broken. Consequences in this classroom will be commensurate—that means they will have something to do with the rule that has been broken. For instance, if one of you decided to dump out the wastebasket on to the floor, what do you think would be a commensurate consequence?"

Listen to responses, giving them feedback on their comments. Then say "There will be a second part to consequences in this classroom. I want to help you remember the rules, but I also always want you to feel good about who you are and to know that I want you to succeed. Because that is important to me, I will make sure that the consequences you experience will not embarrass you. In your small groups, please spend the next five minutes brainstorming what would and what would not be embarrassing. It is important for me to hear how you feel about this, so I can make decisions you will be comfortable with if there is a problem."

Let students brainstorm in their groups for the next five minutes. Get the class back together. Put two categories on the board—"Embarrassing" and "Not Embarrassing." List the students' ideas under the proper categories.

Continue by saying "If the time comes that a consequence is necessary, I will talk privately with the student who has broken a rule. Together we will discuss the commensurate and compatible parts of the consequence."

Why Should We Assume Responsibility for Ourselves?
—By Margaret Abbott—

Age group:
4th-6th grade.

Objective:
To communicate with students the value and empowerment of assuming responsibility for their own actions and learning.

Time:
30 minutes.

Materials:
Poster board and felt pens.

Procedure:
Begin by asking students "What are you responsible for when you are in school?" Accept any and all responses. Then ask "When are you responsible for yourselves at school?" Allow for many responses, then ask "When are you not responsible for yourselves?"

Give them time to think and respond. Work to bring a focus on the idea that the adults in school only have to be responsible for students who get hurt or are not able to take care of themselves. Finally ask "Would you rather be responsible for yourself, or have someone responsible for you?" Encourage responses working toward consensus on being responsible for themselves.

Ask students "Why do you want to be responsible for yourself?" Put their reasons on poster board under the label of "We want to be responsible for ourselves because..."

Adaptation for Younger Students:
Ask student to draw a picture of what they do on their own at school. Share the pictures and lead a discussion on doing things for themselves. Use the word "responsible," but first check to make sure they understand its meaning. Make a language experience chart using their lists of what they are responsible for on one side, and put their ideas of when the teacher needs to be responsible for them on the other side.

Example of Language Experience Chart:

"I'm in charge when.....	"My teacher is in charge when...
I do my work	I get hurt
Walk in the hall	I hurt someone else
Play at recess	I take something that is not mine
Share my things	
Listen to a story	
Draw at my desk	

Due Process:

The Concepts of Notice, Fair Hearing, and Appeal
—By Margaret Abbott—

Due Process

Age group:
3rd to 6th grade.

Objectives:
To familiarize students with the ways in which Due Process can be practiced in the schools. To keep the students cognizant of the responsibility they have to follow the process when they disagree with an adult.

Time:
45 minutes.

Materials:
Three worksheets—samples of which are included with this series of lesson plans.

Procedure:
Begin by asking "What are the three components of Due Process? Does Due Process enter into our school day? How do we use Due Process with our rules and how does it help with consequences? Let's look at the first step in Due Process, called 'Notice.' Here are three worksheets on Due Process Notice, Due Process Hearing, and Due Process Appeal."

Ask the students to work through all three sheets individually and write down the answers they believe to be most appropriate. As each sheet is completed, have the students check their answers with a partner, then move on to the next worksheet. While the students are working, move around the room listening for any signs of misunderstanding or confusion. Keep account of those misunderstandings to discuss with the class when they finish this task. When they are finished, begin a discussion of each component of Due Process. Base your discussion questions on the dialogue you overheard as the students were working.

Be sure to cover the following points with the students: What if we did not have Due Process in school? What does Due Process protect? Do you have Due Process at home? Does the Constitution promise Due Process at home? Can you explain time, place, and manner in your own words? Why is it important to consider time, place, and manner when you disagree with someone? Does Due Process mean that you can break a law if you don't like it?

Worksheet #1

Due Process—Notice

List the rules your class will have during the school year.
Give a defense for each rule.

1.

2.

3.

4.

Worksheet #2

Due Process—Hearing

What can you do if you believe that you have been given a consequence for a rule you didn't break?

Give three examples of the appropriate:

Time:

Place:

Manner:

Worksheet #3

Due Process—Appeal

For what reason might you appeal the decision of a teacher or school official?
Include in your explanation:

     When you might appeal;

     Where you would appeal;

     And how you would appeal.

In what order would you appeal to the following people if you disagree with the decision of a teacher?
Mark your choices in a 1, 2, 3 order:

_____ Superintendent/School Board

_____ Principal

_____ Parent

Due Process—Notice

Age group:
3rd to 6th grade.

Objective:
To inform students of the components of due process. To create simulation exercises that provide students with the opportunity to apply the concepts in practice.

Time:
30 minutes.

Materials:
Butcher paper. Examples of ads and notices.

Procedure:
Explain that "Due Process, granted to us under the Fourteenth Amendment, gives us freedom with certain responsibilities. Let's divide into our groups of four and look at Due Process more carefully. We will begin with 'Notice.'"

Divide the class into groups of four or five students. Give each group an example of notices that you have collected or prepared, such as: Contest applications with the rules listed, a notice for a lost pet, classroom rules, a For Sale ad, chores at home, bike safety rules, paper route job description, etc.

Ask students to discuss within their groups why each notice is of importance. Before they begin, hand out a copy of the following list of questions to guide their discussions:

       1. What if these notices were not given?
       2. What sort of information is given in each notice?
       3. Is the notice important? Why or why not?

Have each group report their conclusions.

On a piece of butcher paper, have the students make a list of the purposes or importance of notices. (You may wish to guide them through this process.) Only statements of consensus should be included on the butcher paper.

Due Process—Hearing

Age group:
3rd to 6th grade.

Objective:
To assist students in their understanding of how Due Process applies to their lives and specifically to classroom interactions.

Time:
30 minutes.

Materials:
Notice examples described below.

Procedure:
Using the examples presented under "Notice," give each group of four students a scenario with a problem to solve.

Examples:

1. Disneyland contest application indicates that you have to be 18 years to enter, but you enter anyway and win. Would you want a hearing? Who would you want to talk to about winning the contest?

2. You see a notice about a lost puppy in the neighborhood. When walking home from school, you see a puppy and the puppy follows you home. The puppy matches the description of the lost dog, but it also looks underfed and neglected. Would you want a hearing? Who would you talk to about finding the puppy?

3. One of the chores on your list at home is taking out the garbage every day. You've been really good about doing that chore for three months, but you are getting tired of it. Would you want a hearing? Who would you want to talk to about "garbage detail?"

4. The class rules are posted in the classroom, but you don't understand why there is a rule about talking in class. You like to visit with a neighbor while you work and you always complete your work on time. Would you want a hearing? Who would you need to talk to about the rule?

5. You have a paper route and the job description says that you must deliver to every house daily. At one house, there is a big dog that snaps at you and barks, but it is only there on the weekends. You decide not to deliver the paper on Sundays. Your manager finds out you aren't delivering the paper and fires you. Would you want a hearing? Who would you want to talk to about the rule?

6. Bike safety was part of the agreement when you got your first bike. Your parents told you to follow the rules of bike safety, or you would lose the privilege of your bike for awhile. You and a friend decided to take turns riding your bike one day. Your friend rode on the sidewalk and almost ran into a neighbor. The neighbor reported this to your parents and, as promised, your bike is taken away. Would you want to have a hearing? Who would you want to talk to about the bike privileges?

7. A skateboard is advertised in the paper "for sale in good condition." You really want one. You ride your bike all the way across town to check it out. When you get there, they show you an old, cracked, and broken skateboard for $10. Would you want a hearing? With whom would you want to talk about the information in the ad?

Give each group a chance to discuss the scenario and arrive at some possible solutions. Each group should also decide with whom they might want to discuss the problem. The next step is to have the groups take turns explaining the problem as they see it. Then each group should be prepared to name who would be the best person to hear the problem. (Remind them that they need to consider who has the authority to grant a solution.) Groups would also need to be prepared to tell what solutions they think could be given.

Have the class determine some guidelines to follow if they were to find themselves in similar situations. Be sure that if the concepts of time, place, and manner do not appear in their thinking, that you guide them through those concepts and clarify as necessary:

> What are appropriate times for a hearing?
> When would be an appropriate time for a hearing?
> What is an appropriate manner for discussing the problem?

Closing:
Assure your students that they are entitled to a hearing in all situations in school, just as adults are in society. Tell them if consequences are ever necessary, they will always have the rights to a hearing first.

Due Process—Appeal

Age group:
3rd to 6th grade.

Objectives:
To help students understand the appeal process and how it pertains to classroom decisions.

Time:
40 minutes.

Materials:
Situations used in the lesson on "Hearing."

Procedure:
As a class, choose one of the scenarios from the previous lesson to try in "court." Cast one student each in the roles of attorneys, judge, and recorder. The teacher should assume the role of clerk to call the court to order. The rest of the students will be the jury, unless either side desires specific students to be witnesses.

Each person would be given about ten minutes to plan their part, while the teacher uses that time to instruct the judge and jurors in their responsibilities.

The court should then be called to session by the teacher. The judge and jury should be given 15-20 minutes to hear the case and determine whether to hold with the hearing decision, or overturn it in favor of a new decision.

Closing:
Discuss with the class when they would feel it necessary to appeal a decision made by the teacher. Ask them to make a list of the people to whom they would make an appeal if they disagreed with a decision made by an adult in the school.

Tell them that it is important to understand with whom they can appeal a decision they believe is unfair. Assure them that they can always appeal a teacher's decision and that it is their right to do so.

Rights and Responsibilities:

Three Lessons Using *A Children's Book* by James Clavell
—By Betty Powers—

Lesson One

Age Group:
5th to 7th grade.

Objectives:
1. To introduce students to the concept of citizenship and the idea that a citizen has responsibilities as well as rights.
2. After reading *A Children's Story* by James Clavell to the students they will be able to choose eight events in the story and decide if they were similar or different from their own school experiences.

Time:
45 minutes.

Materials:
A Children's Story by James Clavell and copies of Worksheet One.

Procedure:
Open by asking the students what they think citizenship is. Give the students time to think about it and respond. After the students have given their ideas, introduce a definition of citizenship as possessing the rights and duties of a citizen.

After they have some basic understanding of citizenship, pass out the worksheet and explain: "The story we are going to read is about the first day of school for some other students. As you listen to the story you are going to write down eight events that the new teacher in the story does differently from the original teacher, Miss Worden. Do not write anything down until I ask you to begin. One event has already been done for you.

Read *A Children's Story* up to the first event on the sheet. Help the students review the two different approaches of the teachers and remind them to listen and pick seven more ways in which the teachers are different from each other. Continue reading the story to its completion. The book takes about twenty-five minutes to read.

As a class discuss the setting and the main characters and fill in the top part of the worksheet together. It is inferred from the story that the setting is in the United States at the end of a war which our country lost. The main characters are the new teacher and Johnny. Give the students time to confer with each other. Have students work in groups of four to review the story and select the remaining seven events. Finally, have the groups engage in discussions to compare each of their events with what they would expect to happen in a classroom. If they think the event might happen, they should write "yes" next to the line on the worksheet. If they think it would not happen, they should write down "no." Do the first one together as a whole class to model what they are to do.

Closure:

Discuss the idea that some things in the story are very different from what happens in our classroom. We have certain rights that are guaranteed to protect us from wrong or unfair behavior. Tomorrow we will discuss some of the differences between events in the story and our school. We will look at the laws we have that protect us from unfair practices.

Worksheet One

Setting _____

_____

Main Characters _____

_____

As you listen to the story, make notes concerning the ways in which the new teacher differs from the original teacher, Miss Worden. Prepare to share your notes and fill in the worksheet with your group when the story is over.

1. Memorized the students' names _____

2. _____

3. _____

4. _____

5. _____

6. _____

7. _____

8. _____

Lesson Two

Objectives:
1. To introduce the students to the rights they have as guaranteed in the First, Fourth, and Fourteenth Amendments.
2. To encourage the students to apply what is in the amendments to classroom situations from *A Children's Story* and current events.

Time:
45 minutes.

Materials:
A Children's Story by James Clavell, completed worksheet from Lesson One, copies of the First, Fourth, and Fourteenth Amendments, activity sheet, large sheet of drawing paper, and markers or crayons.

Procedure:
Divide the class into three groups. Give each group one of the amendments to study and a large piece of drawing paper. As each group discusses their amendment, circulate through the room to make sure they clearly understand the language and meaning of the amendments. (Jigsaw learning can be employed here to allow the various groups to peer teach their information to members of other groups.) Each group will discuss and report back to class on what is in the amendment that protects them. On the large piece of drawing paper, they should visually give clues that will help the class remember what is in their group's amendment. This can be a drawing, jingle, or something else that will help other students remember the contents of the amendments. (20-25 minutes)

Have each group report back to the class and explain their visual clues. Put the main ideas on the board. Lead the class in a discussion of the three amendments presented.

Finally, using Worksheet One from *A Children's Story*, have the students compare the items marked with "no" to one of the three amendments. For example, one event they may have listed on their paper as something that would not happen at school is the teacher giving all the student olive-colored clothing to wear. This can be contrasted to the First Amendment, which has been interpreted to guarantee freedom of expression. Have the students write the matching amendment number to the left of events that were marked "no." Use the remainder of the time to discuss the events and the rights of the students that were protected or violated in the story.

Extended Activity:
Have the students find a newspaper article that deals with one of the discussed amendments and tell what happened, which freedom was involved, and if the person's rights were protected. (See Worksheet Two.)

Worksheet Two

Find a newspaper article that deals with one of the following guaranteed freedoms:

Freedom of speech.
Freedom of religion.
Freedom of the press.
Freedom of peaceful assembly.
Freedom from unreasonable search and seizure.
A person cannot be denied life, liberty, or property without
        due process.
All persons are entitled to equal protection under the law.

Attach your article to this worksheet, then complete the following:

What happened? _____

_____

_____

What right does this involve? _____

_____

_____

Were the person's rights protected? _____

Explain _____

_____

_____

_____

Lesson Three

Objectives:
1. To encourage the students to evaluate their rights and associated responsibilities that go with them.
2. To introduce under what conditions the students' rights give way to the majority. (Compelling State Interests)
3. To have students apply their new knowledge of individual rights to given situations requiring decision making about what action should be taken.

Time:
45 minutes.

Materials:
Two word strips for each student, copies of the decision worksheets for each student.

Procedure:
Review the rights previously presented and write them on the board or on an overhead. Recall the idea from the first day that when one has rights one also has responsibilities. Pass out two word strips to each student. On one have them write down one of the guaranteed rights. On the other word strip have them write down a responsibility that goes with the right.

For example: Right—freedom of the press; Responsibility—to report accurately, don't lie. Lead a class discussion on several rights and their balancing responsibilities. Collect the word strips when everyone is finished. You can go over them in class or use them as part of a bulletin board designed to remind students not only of their rights but the responsibilities as well.

Introduce the concept that on specific occasions a student's rights may be lost. Rights can be lost when the state, or in this case a teacher, can show a Compelling State Interest. The Compelling State Interests are: Property loss and damage; Legitimate Educational Purpose; Health and Safety; and Serious Disruption of the Educational Process. Write them on the board, and have the students brainstorm examples of situations that might involve the four interests. Talk about rules the classroom should have based on these interests. Lead students in a large-group discussion to develop class rules based on the concept of rights balanced with responsibilities. (Alternatively, you can have students work through this part of the lesson in small groups.)

Extended Activity:
Have the class break up into small groups. Give each group copies of Worksheet Three, "What Are The Issues?" Have them come up with one or more possible solutions to the problems presented.

Closure:
Discuss with the class some of the solutions the groups came up with. Then open the discussion to the class as to why there must be a balance of rights and responsibilities. It is important, as a citizen, to know their rights and how they can be responsible. This knowledge can help them to become better citizens and protect their freedoms.

Worksheet Three

What Are the Issues?

You are a Supreme Court judge. What decision would you give? What would be your explanation? What are the issues?

1. The Constitution gives us freedom of speech. During a speech people in the audience start to heckle the person talking. They become so loud that no one can hear the speaker. What are the rights of: the hecklers, the speaker, the rest of the audience? What are the issues?

_____

_____

2. Two students in a class start rumors about another student in class. When confronted, they say their freedom of speech allows them to spread the rumors, whether or not they are true. What are the issues?

_____

_____

3. The Constitution guarantees freedom of the press. Students complain that some of their newspaper articles are being censored or severely edited. They say this violates their rights. What are the issues?

_____

_____

4. A student wears a shirt to school with offensive language on it. A school official asks the student to take it off. The student says that wearing the shirt is a protected right. What are the issues?

_____

_____

Community Citizenship
—By Betty Powers—

(*Judicious Discipline* can and should extend from the classroom out into the community. One way to facilitate this is by organizing clubs whose purpose it to help students become involved in community projects. Learning tolerance and how to make responsible decisions becomes very relevant when students are faced with real situations.)

Age Group:
4th through 6th graders. (This would be very appropriate for other grades as well.)

Goal:
To broaden the students' concepts of responsible classroom citizenship to include participatory community citizenship.

Objectives:
Students will:
1. Acquire an understanding of, and interest in, their local community.
2. Develop and organize community service projects.
3. Cultivate a feeling of commitment to their community.
4. Heighten their sense of civic ethics.
5. Generate active and responsible civic behavior and involvement in local issues.

Procedure:
The club has two levels of service. At one level the club sponsors school-wide activities as they become aware of local needs. These might include winter clothing drives, canned food drives, packing a pencil box for other students, writing to people in military service or in nursing homes, and staging school-wide clean ups.

Educators should also assist students to feel directly involved as much as is possible given health and safety considerations. In order to achieve this, offer a variety of small group projects in the fall and again in the spring. Have students sign up for the project they would most like to work on each term. Project planning meetings can be held after school or during class time, depending on school rules and the extent of student involvement. It is important to let students have sufficient time to talk about their projects and experiences.

Projects:
Communities seem to dictate to some degree the type of projects that are needed. What follows is a list of some that we have carried out in our school:

Pack a Pencil Box:

School pencil boxes were purchased and distributed to the homeroom teachers. (Fund raisers can be held during the year to cover expenses for any unusual materials; our own budget typically runs about $300 per year.) Students were asked to donate new items that are used at school and/or spare change. At the end of the month the filled boxes were collected. The money collected was used to provide any items still needed for the school boxes as well as notebook paper. The boxes were donated to the local women's shelter for children who were starting school in a new place and who had no supplies.

Winter Clothing Drive:

This type of project is especially necessary where winters are very cold. Items of clothing can be distributed to a number of different organizations that help people in need.

Activity Boards:

These toys are made from patterns for a quiet book. Students attached flannel pieces, "googly" eyes, and ribbons to tag board. The toys help small children learn to tie, button, and braid.

Books:

Students created their own stories as part of a small-group activity. The stories were written, illustrated, and bound with spiral backs. Students donated their books to different organizations working with children.

Work Projects:

Local needs should always be a prime consideration when identifying projects. Our students have worked at a nature center, helped to put in flower beds at a local park, planted and tended flowers around our school, and helped with other specific projects assigned by the school custodian.

Gifts:

At different times during the year, students have donated between 200 to 300 small items to be passed out to the children at the Ronald McDonald Pediatric Clinic. Students made some of the items listed above for this project.

Senior Lunches:

Our students have two places within walking distance that provide lunches for senior citizens. Students have decorated tables, provided entertainment, and helped to serve the meals.

Decorations:

Students use their creative talents to brighten up shelters, clinics, and senior residences.

Since the inception of the clubs, students and community members have been able to work together to make our community one in which we are all proud to live

Point of View/Conflict Resolution

(This lesson plan, which accompanies the dual picture of the old and young women on the following page, was developed as experimental material by the School Initiatives Program operating in conjunction with the Community Board Center for Policy and Training in San Francisco, California. It is reprinted here with their permission.)

Age group:
3rd through 6th grade.

Objectives:
To promote awareness of how perceptual limitations can affect communication. To promote acceptance of divergent points of view.

Time:
10 to 15 minutes.

Materials:
Transparency of young girl/old woman drawing and/or one copy for each student.

Procedure:
Show picture of young girl/old woman to the group. Ask students to describe what they see in the picture. Assist students who have difficulty identifying both aspects of the drawing. [Editor's note: I have found it useful to have students trace both faces on the picture for other students who can see only one of the faces.] Expand the discussion to other areas in which a person's point of view might be limited by his/her perception of information. Ask students how this activity could be useful to them in various curriculum areas.

Process Questions:
Why did some people see a young woman while others saw an old woman?
Is there a "correct" way to see the picture?
Is anybody able to see both aspects simultaneously?
How might interpersonal conflicts result from individuals perceiving information differently?
How might such conflicts be resolved?
What did you feel towards those who saw the drawing the same way you did?
Towards those who saw it differently?
What did you feel when you "discovered" the other aspect of the picture?

Citizenship:
A Middle Grades Language Arts Lesson Plan
—By Bill Lee—

Age Group:
7th grade.

Objective:
Students will be able to explain their rights as United States citizens as provided by the Fourteenth Amendment's Equal Protection Clause.

Time:
40 to 50 minutes.

Materials:
The Classroom Citizenship Test (which follows on next page), paper and writing instrument, copy of the Fourteenth Amendment.

Procedure:
Teacher will ask students to prepare for a citizenship test. Tell students that if they were not born in this country, they would have to take a test as part of the requirement for citizenship. The test may be given orally or as a handout.

Ask students to check their answers once the test has been completed. Read off the correct answers. Students should check their own work. Ask students how they felt about their understanding of the test items.

Ask students to imagine with you that the rest of their educational year depended on how they had answered the test questions. "Suppose I said to you that those of you who missed more than two questions would have your citizenship taken away, and you would not be entitled to an education in this school." Go on to imagine that students who answered 18 or more correctly would be entitled to special privileges. Ask students if there is anything wrong with that. Students will probably respond that they have "rights."

Read the Fourteenth Amendment to them. Discuss each right provided by the amendment and give examples of how it impacts our everyday lives. Explain to students that we will discuss the rights provided by the Amendment in more detail later, but to realize that their citizenship rights can not be taken away from them. They will always be citizens no matter what happens.

The Classroom Citizenship Test

This test is to be used with the lesson on the previous page:

Questions:

1. Name the Viking explorer who many believe "discovered" America long before Christopher Columbus did.
2. Which country financed Columbus' voyage to America?
3. Why is Amerigo Vespucci important to American history?
4. Which country ruled the American Colonies in the middle 1700s?
5. Name the British law which taxed lead, paint, paper, and tea imported into the colonies.
6. What was the last major battle of the American Revolution?
7. Which was the first state to ratify the Constitution?
8. What do we call the first 10 Amendments of the Constitution?
9. From which country did the United States make the Louisiana Purchase?
10. What country fought against the United States during the War of 1812.
11. The Woman's Rights convention was held in 1848. In which city did this event take place?
12. What was the Abolition movement?
13. How many states seceded from the Union during the Civil War?
14. Who was the president during the Civil War?
15. Which amendment to the Constitution gave women the right to vote?
16. What did the 18th Amendment do?
17. When did the Great Depression take place.
18. What was the "New Deal"?
19. Why is the date December 7th, 1941, important in U.S. history?
20. Who delivered the "I Have A Dream" speech on the steps of the Lincoln Memorial?

Answers:

1. Lief Ericson.
2. Spain.
3. America was named after him.
4. England.
5. The Townshend Acts.
6. The Battle of Yorktown.
7. Delaware.
8. The Bill of Rights.
9. France.
10. England.
11. Seneca Falls, New York.
12. A movement to end slavery.
13. Eleven.
14. Abraham Lincoln.
15. The 19th Amendment.
16. Prohibited the sale of alcoholic beverages nationwide, later repealed by the 21st Amendment.
17. 1930s.
18. Presidejnt Franklin D. Roosevelt's program of economic recovery from the Great Depression.

19. The date the Japanese bombed Pearl Harbor and the United States entered World War II.
20. Dr. Martin Luther King, Jr.

Crossword Puzzle:
A Judicious Discipline Enrichment Activity
—By Bill Lee—

The crossword puzzle on the following page was developed for use as an enrichment activity for intermediate and middle level students working with *Judicious Discipline*.

The word list for the puzzle answers are as follows:

Amendment
Balance
Bill of Rights
Choice
Compelling Interests
Consequences
Constitution
Due Process
Equality
Freedom
Fulcrum
Judicious Discipline
Justice
Liberty
Life
Property
Responsibilities
Rewards
Rights
You

ACROSS

1. Balances the rights of the individual with those of the group; based on the Constitution.
3. An added section of the U.S. Constitution.
5. The balancing point.
7. Provided by the 14th Amendment.
8. The key to making Judicious Discipline work in the classroom
9. The backbone of Judicious Discipline.
10 Free will.
11. The duties of a citizen.
15. The quality or state of being free.
18. Existence.
19. The gifts of the U.S. Constitution.
20. The Law of the Land.

DOWN

2. The rights of the state or group which outweigh the rights of the individual; laws or rules.
4. Fair treatment under the law.
6. The results of negative actions or behavior.
12. What you or someone else owns.
13. The first Ten Amendments to the Constitution.
14. To do as you feel.
16. The results of positive actions or behavior.
17. Measuring everyone with the same yardstick.

Prejudice Boxes

—By Bill Lee—

(This lesson was developed to enrich students' experience when reading *The Outsiders*. It may also be used as part of a unit on human relationships and peer interaction.)

Age group:
Intermediate.

Objectives:
The students will develop the ability to:
1) Discriminate the factors of prejudice by analyzing its cause.
2) Explain character actions by identifying their motives.
3) Understand their human relation skills by examining their interactions with others.

Time:
40 to 50 minutes.

Materials:
Twenty boxes (shoe boxes are too small, you will need the sort of box that might be found in grocery stores); word strips; markers; and pen and paper

Procedure:
Divide the classroom with a taped line on the floor. Place four or five desks along the line. Separate the class into two equal groups. (One idea for dividing them up might be a preference for one or another brand of soft drink, or have them draw strips of colored paper such as red and blue. Do not use personal attributes.) Have students list differences between the two groups and develop a list to describe both groups.

Alternating between groups; have each read the list of differences generated. (Be careful, this may turn into a free-for-all, if not controlled.) Write down the differences cited by the two groups. After a substantial list has been created, have the students turn their chairs so the two groups are facing each other.

Condense the comments into one- or two-word category descriptors. For instance, "All people with red paper are strange" could become "generalizations." Record your category descriptors onto the word strips, and tape the strips to the boxes—one per box. Pile the boxes on top of the desks between the two groups. Continue this until all the boxes are stacked up.

(It is strongly suggested that you prepare a list of characteristics dealing with prejudice for this lesson. I have done the lesson with and without a set list; with the list is better because you can add in the words the students don't name.)

Ask one person to describe another person from the opposite group. Because the view will be blocked by boxes, this will be difficult to do. Ask two or three other students to describe each other until they realize that, like these boxes, prejudice hinders our view of others.

Have the students copy the words listed on the boxes. Tell them that in order to remove the boxes, we must find the opposites of these words. (love/hate, ignorance/knowledge, etc.) As the boxes are removed, have students write the new words next to their antonyms.

English as a Second Language:
Two Worksheets
—By Juanita Weber-Shirk—

Worksheet One

Which Individual Right Is Illustrated In Each Of The Following Examples?

1. When Sisavath is giving a report about Laos, the teacher tells him not to say anything good about the communist government.

_____

_____

2. When Thanh gets a message that some more of her family have left Vietnam by boat, the teacher asks the class to stop their work and pray for the safety of Thanh's family.

_____

_____

3. The students from Ms. Dwyer's class decide to study together for a large unit test. They meet after school in the park across from the public library. They have been studying for about one half hour, causing no disruptions, when a policeman tells them that they must go somewhere else to work.

_____

_____

4. A new student gets involved in a fight and is suspended immediately. She doesn't get a chance to explain what happened, or to ask that the suspension be dropped.

_____

_____

5. Luis cannot see the chalkboard from his seat in the back of the classroom. He gets a bad grade on a quiz because he could not read the questions on the board and the teacher told him not to move out of his seat one more time.

_____

_____

6. Mrs. Weber-Shirk cannot find her keys. She asks every student to open his or her backpack and she looks in all of them for her keys.

_____

_____

Worksheet Two

Which Compelling State Interest Is Illustrated In Each Of The Following Examples?

1. Ms. Clark will not let students jump through the windows into the courtyard. She makes them go out through the door.

_____

2. Ms. White requires students to return the Global Studies textbooks at the end of the school year.

_____

3. In the middle of a unit on sea life, the students ask to see the movie *Teenage Mutant Ninja Turtles*. Ms. Dwyer turns down the request.

_____

4. Students must get certain immunizations and vaccinations in order to stay in school.

_____

5. Ms. White does not permit students to wear headsets while she lectures.

_____

6. Ms. Weber-Shirk will not let students write on desks or walls in her classroom.

_____

7. Students walking in the hallways during the time classes are in session are required to be quiet.

_____

Integrating Mathematics with Judicious Discipline
—By Jane Richards—

(Begin introducing the concepts of Mathematics integrated with **Judicious Discipline** by using ideas from the following discussion suggestions.)

When approaching a mathematical problem that needs to be solved, before we begin making decisions, we need to look at what we're "given." Sometimes we're given information in a word problem, restrictions on a variable (e.g., if $1/x$ is a real number, x cannot equal 0), something to graph—there are a lot of possibilities. We need to think about how the givens affect the approach we choose in solving a problem. We need to think about what the problems ask us to do or find out. Even when there seems to be an "obvious" way to go about solving it, what would happen if we make another choice? Is one decision better than another? Why? Is it faster, easier, or the only one that is mathematically valid? Suppose we get stuck, what are the options open to us? Is it better to try something and risk making a mistake or to give up? Why? Where could we go or who could we ask for help if we need it? Have other people tried to solve a similar problem? Did they find a solution? Does it make sense? Did we arrive at the same conclusions? How would we approach this type of situation next time?

Why are there rules? What mathematical "rules" can we think of? (Properties of each operation, properties of equality, geometric properties, etc.) Suppose we applied our problem-solving skills to analyze decisions we make when we form policies for our classroom. What are our "givens?"

Family values—rules, priorities, expectations
School policies
District policies
State Education Department policies
Laws
U.S. Constitution

[Editor's Note: At this point Ms. Richards leads her students through an overview of **Judicious Discipline**.]

Mathematicians often use a flow chart to graphically show how to make decisions and what the consequences of the decisions are. (Give examples. Discuss, review, or introduce flow charts.) How could we incorporate this into making positive decisions in our classroom?

Activity:

Engage students in brainstorming rules for the class based on the Compelling State Interests. What particular areas might require special attention?

Homework
Contribution to your grade
Timeliness of arrival to class
Completing assignments on time
Classroom behavior

Divide the class into groups and have each group devise a flow chart for a specific area that needs to be explored. Encourage students to include consequences for making decisions that are different from the ones the groups decide to choose as "best."

[Editor's Note: What follows are two possible flow charts that might be devised by students. After the flow charts is a worksheet that would apply to any flow chart developed.]

Flow Chart One:
Homework

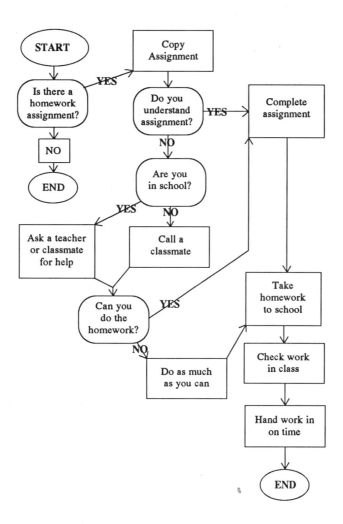

Flow Chart Two:
Arriving Late to Class

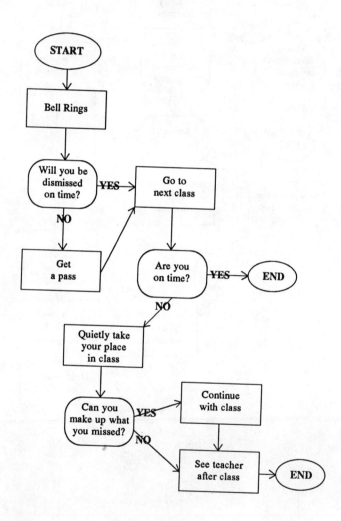

Worksheet

What is the Compelling State Interest involved?

_____

_____

What decisions are to be made

_____

_____

How do the "givens" affect this process?

_____

_____

What do you consider the best decisions to be and why?

_____

_____

Do your choices match the four Compelling State Interests?

_____

How?

_____

_____

Check top make sure you have considered alternatives to the option you consider to be the most appropriate and have included consequences to those decisions.

Working to Solve Problems

(Editor's Note: The following items are examples of rules and consequences developed at schools employing *Judicious Discipline*. The emphasis in each case is on problem solving and not punishments. The problem-solving worksheets should never be used without adult supervision, adult input, and a one-on-one problem-solving session with the student afterwards. Some teachers encourage their students to draw the problem, an appropriate alternative for any age group.)

South Elementary School Student Management Plan
St. Peter, Minnesota

Self Discipline is our goal for all students at South Elementary. We want students to develop responsibility for themselves and their own actions. We believe that if a student infringes upon the rights of others there must be fair and consistent consequences for that action. We do not want anyone to interrupt or prevent our students from learning. We strive to teach self-discipline by reasoning, discussing alternative behavior, and attempting to deal with each problem in a fair and consistent manner. Our faculty and staff realize that everyone makes mistakes, but our goal is to help students learn from their mistakes so they are less likely to repeat them. We attempt to treat each student with the dignity and respect [each] deserve[s] during that teaching process.

Our ultimate goal is to prepare students to be contributing members of a society which uses a democratic process. It is hoped that students who leave South Elementary will possess academic and social skills that will begin to prepare them to function as responsible citizens.

Student responsibilities [are to]:

Act in a safe and healthy way.
Treat all property with respect.
Respect the rights and needs of others.
Take responsibility for learning.

General School Rules

Lacomb Elementary School, Lacomb, Oregon

1. Act In A Safe And Healthy Way.

Be kind with words and actions. Use furniture and equipment appropriately, walk in the building, follow playground rules, follow lunch line rules, follow bus riding rules, keep hands and feet to self.

(Compelling State Interest: Health and Safety.

2. Treat All Property With Respect.

Take care of school property and equipment. Respect and care for the personal property of yourself and others. Borrow property of others only after receiving permission. If you break someone's property, fix or replace it.

(Compelling State Interest: Property Loss and Damage.)

3. Respect Rights And Needs of Others.

Work and play without disrupting others, show courtesy towards others, cooperate to help others learn, use positive words and actions.

(Compelling State Interest: Serious Disruption of the Educational Process.)

4. Take Responsibility For Your Learning.

Work hard and do your best, come to school prepared to learn, be a good listener, turn in your assignments on time, do your homework, have necessary materials, set a good example for others, feel good about yourself, be on time.

(Compelling State Interest: Legitimate Educational Process.)

The staff and students of Lacomb Elementary School developed these general school rules during the Spring of 1992. These rules come from the laws of our nation regarding individual rights, freedoms, and responsibilities to others.

We use an educational approach to discipline, where students learn and practice taking responsibility for their behavior. We teach problem-solving and decision-making skills.

Students are taught their rights and responsibilities as citizens [secured for] them by the Constitution of the United States. They are taught that they lose their individual rights when they take away the rights of others.

The teachers and students of each classroom will write their classroom rules that explain the compelling state interests. Classroom rules will be sent home to parents in October.

What To Do When A Rule Is Broken:
Possible Consequences
South Elementary School, St. Peter, Minnesota

Possible Consequences Could Include:

Self-evaluation/conference form
Apology
Conference with students and/or parents
Restitution
Redoing an assignment
Counseling
School service project
Loss of privileges
Study with a tutor or study-buddy
Time out
Problem solving room
Mediation

Resources Available for Problem Solving:

Teachers
Counselor/Social Worker
Learning Disabilities Teacher
Emotional/Behavioral Disabilities Teacher
Principal
Psychologist
Self-evaluation/conference form

Student Self-Evaluation Form

South Elementary School, St. Peter, Minnesota

Student _____   Date _____

Time _____   Reported by _____

Today I _____

_____

_____

because _____

_____

_____

I did not:

_____ Act in a safe and healthy way

_____ Treat all property with respect

_____ Respect the rights and needs of others

_____ Take responsibility for learning

I should have _____

_____

_____

Student Signature _____

Behavior Form

South Elementary School, St. Peter, Minnesota

Name _____   Date _____

Today I _____

_____

_____

Next time I will try to _____

_____

_____

I will help myself to remember by _____

_____

_____

(After you fill this out, another member of our school community will speak with you about the incident. Thank you for helping us help you to resolve the problem.)

Student Signature _____

Post Conference:

_____ (Student's name) and

I _____ (Problem Solving Partner's name)

spoke about the problem. The following decisions were made:

_____

_____

Notification Slip

—By Betty Powers—

This form was developed to help students remember their assignments. The author reports that as the school year progresses, she has to use this form less and less often. It is designed to inform parents and students about what assignments are missing and/or alternatives the students need to complete. The author reports: "When the parents sign it, and the students return it, I have a record of notification if needed later."

Notification Slip

_____ needs extra help

in_____

He/she may report for help on_____
(Date)

at_____
(Time)

in Room_____

____ He/she may be helped at home.

Assignments:

Comments:

_____   _____
(Teacher)   (Parent or Guardian)

Notification Slip

_____ needs extra help

in_____

He/she may report for help on_____
(Date)

at_____
(Time)

in Room_____

____ He/she may be helped at home.

Assignments:

Comments:

_____   _____
(Teacher)   (Parent or Guardian)

Notification Slip

_____ needs extra help

in_____

He/she may report for help on_____
(Date)

at_____
(Time)

in Room_____

____ He/she may be helped at home.

Assignments:

Comments:

_____   _____
(Teacher)   (Parent or Guardian)

Notification Slip

_____ needs extra help

in_____

He/she may report for help on _____
(Date)

at_____
(Time)

in Room_____

____ He/she may be helped at home.

Assignments:

Comments:

_____   _____
(Teacher)   (Parent or Guardian)

Receipt Form

—By Heidi Weismuller—

Receipts like those on this page should be used with students as recognition of their property rights.

RECEIPT from _____ for _____ Turn this receipt in at the end of the day to have your item returned. Signed _____ Date _____	**RECEIPT** from _____ for _____ Turn this receipt in at the end of the day to have your item returned. Signed _____ Date _____
RECEIPT from _____ for _____ Turn this receipt in at the end of the day to have your item returned. Signed _____ Date _____	**RECEIPT** from _____ for _____ Turn this receipt in at the end of the day to have your item returned. Signed _____ Date _____

An Introductory Letter to Parents and Guardians

—By Heidi Weismuller—

(The following letter was developed for teachers to use in introducing *Judicious Discipline* to parents and guardians.)

Dear Parent or Guardian,

This year I will be using a form of discipline in my classroom called *Judicious Discipline*. As author and educator Forrest Gathercoal states in his book by that title, "*Judicious Discipline* is a disciplinary style and philosophy based on the synthesis of law, education, and ethics. [It] calls for teaching students about their individual rights and freedoms along with their responsibilities to others: in other words, an educational approach," rather than a punitive one. *Judicious Discipline* uses the same system of citizenship rights and responsibilities for classroom governance as we adults live under every day.

Students will be actively involved in determining classroom rules which will be based on four Compelling State Interests. These rules will then be discussed in class and posted in the room as a guideline for maintaining a positive learning environment. The four Compelling State Interests are:

1. Property Loss and Damage
2. Legitimate Educational Purpose
3. Health and Safety
4. Serious Disruption of the Educational Process

Along with making the rules, the students will also be involved in determining possible consequences if the rules are broken. These consequences will have an educational aim and will not be meaningless or humiliating. By being directly involved in the discipline process, students will develop a respect for the rules, and discipline problems should seldom occur.

Assignments which are not completed often pose more of a problem for teachers than for students. Giving students failing grades for incomplete assignments lets the students rightly say "The teacher gave me an 'F.'" However, recording an incomplete until assignments are handed in places the burden of responsibility on the student. I will have two baskets in my room, one for papers handed in on time, and one for papers handed in late. I will correct the papers handed in on time promptly, while I will correct late papers when I have time. Because this could result in an incomplete for the course, I will make every effort to work with the students and with you to help every person in my classroom take the responsibility of handing in assignments on time. I will not give an "F" for a paper not submitted; for many students that would be the easy way out of completing class work.

Students will be informed of these issues during the first week of school. To help you learn more about this form of classroom discipline, I will be holding a meeting on _____ at _____ . I hope you can all attend. If not, please contact me so that we can arrange another time to meet. I would also recommend that you read Gathercoal's *Judicious Discipline* book. If you have any questions concerning these policies, please contact me at _____ at the following times _____ .

Sincerely,

The Fifty-Minute Classroom:
A Suggested Outline for Presenting
Rules and Consequences to Secondary Students
—By Forrest Gathercoal—

1. Briefly review the history of the change from school policies based on the concept of *in loco parentis* to today's need for considering the civil rights of students when developing rules and consequences.

2. Talk about how you will approach rules and consequences. A possible scenario might be to say:

> I believe it is my professional responsibility not only to recognize and respect your rights as a citizen in this classroom, but to help you learn how to live within those rights. Balancing your human rights with society's need for an effective educational environment will form the basis for my classroom rules and decisions.
>
> When it comes to consequences, I will strive to keep them commensurate with your actions and compatible with your need for self-worth and right to educational opportunities. If the time comes when you lose your rights, I will make every effort to be evenhanded as we work through the problem together.

3. Explain that the First, Fourth, and Fourteenth Amendments are those most often applied to student rights and how the four Compelling State Interests come into play to take away those rights. Use examples from your class such as:

> a. Student speech and how it applies to the school dress code.
> b. Students' free exercise of religion and the schools' responsibility not to establish religion.
> c. Student press and the distribution or posting of opinions.
> d. Student searches and the need for reasonable suspicion by school authorities.
> e. The equal protection clause and a student's right to an equal educational opportunity in addition to fair and equal treatment under school rules and decisions.
> f. Due process and a student's right to fair and legal rules, notice, a hearing, and appeal.

By using examples of how our justice system weighs the requisites of managing an effective educational environment against a person's individual rights, students should be able to understand their rights are not a license to do as they please in school.

4. Set forth your ideals about how you view the responsibilities and ethics of professional educators. Some topic ideas to be elaborated upon might be:

a. Student-centered: "I recognize that each of you brings different educational and personal needs to this classroom. My goal is to address your individual needs as often as I am able in an effort to help each of you enjoy education and achieve success in school this year."

b. Positive educational practices: "I would like you to know how I feel about teaching and discipline and where I plan to direct my energies and priorities."

c. List of "Nevers": "Let's talk about what experience has taught me and some things I never want to do."

d. Student ethics: "Now that we have discussed my professional ethics, let's consider the ethics of being a good student, i.e. honesty, promptness, consideration or others, etc."

Judicious Discipline at the Secondary Level

—By Richard Neuman—

What follows is a set of lesson plans that may be used for introducing rights and responsibilities at the secondary level. These lessons were designed to help students understand school district rules as set out in the handbook published by the Beaverton, Oregon, school district. The unit has applicability for implementing *Judicious Discipline* as it clarifies legal issues for secondary students.

These lessons need not be reserved for Homeroom or Social Studies. However, students would not need to have this information presented during each class period. It would be sufficient to present each lesson once, with the concepts reiterated as necessary by other faculty members. As specific concerns arise in a Chemistry lab, on the playing fields, or in a Technology class, they should be addressed by the teacher involved.

[Editor's Note: These lessons require a thorough reading of Forrest Gathercoal's *Judicious Discipline* book before you attempt to use them. The issues dealt with here are subtle; please take the time to read about them and understand them before introducing them to your students.]

It can hardly be argued that either students or teachers shed their constitutional rights to freedom of speech or expression at the schoolhouse gate...
—*Tinker v Des Moines Independent School District*, 393 U.S. 503

Public school pupils shall comply with rules for the government of such schools, pursue the prescribed course of study, use the prescribed textbooks, and submit to the teacher's authority.
—Oregon Regulations Section 339.250

From the Beaverton School District handbook:

To the teacher:

You have been charged with teaching the Beaverton School District "Student Responsibilities and Rights" pamphlet. This should involve activities and discussions of the rights of citizens under the Constitution and their responsibilities in the public school setting. This is an opportunity for students to understand individual freedoms and learn to handle responsibilities. The balance of individual rights and the needs of the majority is at the heart of this unit.

In this unit, teachers and students will learn the language of the law and how it applies to school. The activities involve a great deal of teacher/student and student/student interaction, teaching strategies initially developed in the New American lecture, "Concept Attainment," and "Peer Practice." There is also the use of the cooperative learning strategy from "Teams/Games/Tournaments."

Related issues are grouped according to a general topic for each day. The scenarios should be the basis for discussion covering key concepts or each issue. Some could be used at the beginning of class to introduce a topic. For variety, a scenario could be used in small group discussions or for mini-debates. An emphasis on the balance between rights and responsibilities should be emphasized as should the factors involved in meeting individual rights and societal needs. Continually refer students to the key points of the amendments and Compelling State Interests.

This unit will involve you and your students in questions of responsibilities and rights. Payoffs are great; teachers and students have a solid framework for discipline and shaping classroom rules as well as an appreciation of individual differences.

—Day 1—
Concept Attainment Activity:
Rights and Responsibilities

Teacher Instructions:

In concept attainment, a concept is explained by giving examples of what something is and what it isn't. (It is important that the terms Rights and Responsibilities are not revealed to the students, but that they discern these concepts from the descriptions presented.) Have students generate a list of possible words or phrases to match descriptions as you reveal each row, one at a time. As more information is revealed, students will be better able to identify the concept you are describing.

Rights:

1. Guaranteed by Bill of Rights
2. Your freedoms
3. Ability to enjoy life, liberty, property

4. Something you may do

1. No one can take away
2. Cannot be voted on
3. Not always what the majority thinks is right.
4. Not what you have to do

Responsibilities:

1. Helps people get along
2. Helps maintain order
3. Something you should do

1. Not always doing what you want
2. Someone will expect you to do
3. You may be punished for not doing

—Day 2—
Your Rights:
A New American Lecture (Organizer)

The Framework:
U.S. Constitution:
> —law of the land

Bill of Rights:
> —first 10 amendments
> —cannot be voted on

Other Amendments

Freedom:
> —individual vs group

Justice:
> —fairness
> —due process

Equality:
> —distributing burdens and benefits

First Amendment:
Religion:
> —state cannot establish
> —state cannot prohibit

Free Speech:
> —spoken/written word
> —dress
> —length of hair

Press:
> —publication and distribution on school property

Assembly

Fourth Amendment:
Search and Seizure:
> —against unreasonable searches
> —what is reasonable

Fourteenth Amendment:
Life

Property:
> —all one owns

Liberty:
> —present to future

Due Process:
> —life, liberty, and property cannot be denied without due process
> —Substantive due process:
>> —fair laws

—Procedural due process:
       —notice
       —fair hearing
       —appeal
Equal Protection:
       —sex
       —race
       —national origin
       —handicapped
       —marital status
       —age
       —religion

Activity:

Teacher Instructions:

Have students copy your writing from the board/overhead to the organizer as you lecture and explain. After each heading has been discussed, have students complete the following tasks, writing their responses on the back of the organizer. The tasks may be completed by working in groups.

The Framework:

1. List names for "law of land" and where liberties are found?
2. What three things does the Bill of Rights guarantee?

First Amendment:

1. List four freedoms.
2. Give an example of each.
3. Share with a neighbor.

Fourth Amendment:

1. How is this amendment like the First Amendment?

Fourteenth Amendment:

1. Define substantive and procedural due process.
2. How are your rights like the rules of a baseball game?

—Day 3—
Your Responsibilities:
Compelling State Interests

Rules and regulations are needed to provide structure and organization in schools. List at least 10 rules a teacher or principal has written that you have been asked to follow. Share these with a neighbor and then we will list them on the board.

1. _____

2. _____

3. _____

4. _____

5. _____

6. _____

7. _____

8. _____

9. _____

10. _____

How do you feel about these? Were they necessary? Were they fair?

Rules shouldn't just exist because someone thinks they should; rather they must have a purpose. Educators can prohibit conduct which is detrimental or harmful to the operation of schools when it can be demonstrated that there is a Compelling State Interest to do so.

There are four Compelling State Interests listed in the columns on the next page. We will discuss these. and then you can determine which of the ten rules you listed above fit into which column.

(Note to teachers: After explanation, model by putting one example in each column on a duplicate of the chart found on the next page. Duplicate the chart on an overhead or on poster board. Then have students continue to work in groups. After they understand which rules fit into this pattern and which do not, have them create class rules, one for each of the Compelling State Interests. Come together as a class to put the rules up on butcher paper for a class display.)

Compelling State Interests

Property Loss and Damage	Legitimate Educational Purpose	Health and Safety	Serious Disruption

—Day 4—
Attendance and Enrollment

Key words/concepts:

compulsory
exceptions—the impact of family values
attendance in designated school
educational alternatives

Scenarios:

1. John doesn't want to attend the designated school in his area.

2. The Smiths do not want their children taking a sex education course.

3. John and Mary Jones want their child to attend a private school.

4. Cynthia is not given credit for a course because she missed fifteen class periods.

In groups, have the students discuss the scenarios. What rights do the students have in these situations? What are the Compelling State Interests? Which way should the balance tip—in favor of the student or the public school? These questions should be used for this activity and each subsequent activity in this unit.

—Day 5—
Equality of Opportunity

Key words/Concepts:

Fourteenth Amendment
discrimination
handicaps
grievance procedures

Scenarios:

1. In seventh grade, boys who register for applied arts take Wood Shop while girls who register for the same course take Home Economics.

2. In Mr. Brown's class, girls may go to the lavatory without asking for permission, but boys need a hall pass to go.

3. John, a blind student, is not allowed to take shop because he might injure himself.

4. Mrs. White has her three students from Vietnam sit together so that they can help each other.

5. John, a student, got married over spring vacation. The principal of John's school has decided that John must drop out to support his wife.

6. Mr. Green, the counselor, suggested Martha take an English elective instead of math because she'd be the only girl is the class.

Use the questions from the previous activity to respond to the above scenarios.

—Day 6—
Classroom Behavior

Key words/concepts:

positive academic environment
serious disruption to the educational process
plagiarism
appropriate disciplinary action

(refer back to list of rules)

Scenarios:

1. Jeff complains when Mr. King asks him to stop talking during a reading period.

2. Joe is sent to the hallway when Megan complains that he is bothering her.

3. For chewing gum, Jane must stay after school for three consecutive afternoons.

4. Ms. Jones requires Sarah to take a test again when she is caught cheating.

5. For being tardy ten times, Sam's grade is lowered.

6. Jason hasn't brought a pencil to class for the fifth time and is given an "F" on the day's test.

—Day 7—
Student Dress and Grooming

Key words/concepts:

First Amendment
dress code
health and safety
serious disruption of the educational process
property loss and damage

Scenarios:

1. Joe is upset because he lost his shop safety glasses and Mr. Smith, his shop teacher, won't let him operate the power machinery.

2. Ms. Atkins, the principal, has announced a school-wide policy of "no hats."

3. Short skirts are prohibited from all school functions.

4. All high school boys are required to be clean-shaven.

5. Jane doesn't like the blue graduation gowns and decides to wear a red one instead.

6. Adam gets angry when he is told by a teacher that he must wear gym shoes on the gym floor.

—Day 8—
Search and Seizure

Key words/concepts:

Fourth Amendment
seizure
expectancy of privacy
probable cause
health and safety emergency
a search related in scope to the circumstance
blanket search
strip search
illegal act
injurious

Scenarios:

1. The principal searches a student's locker without permission after a teacher reports hearing that drugs might be in there.

2. At the end of the semester, the librarian opens all lockers looking for over-due books. Students have not been notified that the search would occur.

3. When Ms. Tucker discovers a book is missing, she searches all students individually before allowing them to leave the room.

4. A bomb threat has been phoned to the school; all lockers are opened and inspected.

5. All students are asked to empty their pockets and show the contents of all sacks and bags as they enter on the last day of school.

6. The principal suspects Joe has drugs inside his clothes and conducts a strip search.

7. The principal suspects a student has cigarettes inside her purse, but she refuses to let him search for them. The principal calls the student's parents who give permission for the search.

—Day 9—
Suspension and Expulsion

Key words/concepts:

suspension
expulsion
procedural due process
substantive due process
fair hearing
counsel
cross examination
prognosis for rehabilitation

Scenarios

1. The vice-principal sends Sally to in-school suspension for two days. She decides not to tell her parents.

2. Don is suspended until his parents come in for a conference.

3. Marlene is suspended for having cigarettes at the school dance.

4. In December the vice-principal suspends a student for the rest of the school year.

5. John will not graduate because he has been expelled and cannot attend classes.

6. Jason's parents requested a hearing and the hearings officer decide to expel Jason. Jason's parents don't like the decision.

—Day 10—
Freedom of Expression

Key words/concepts:

libel
slander
pervasive vulgarity
Federal Equal Access Act
procedural due process
insubordination
public display of affection
time, place, manner
tolerance
prior restraint

Scenarios:

1. A teacher tells a student that she won't be allowed to give her oral report on "How Communism Has Helped China."

2. Jane is given detention because she called her teacher a "bitch."

3. Frank and Sally are suspended from school because they were kissing in the hallway.

4. Tom is asked to remove his "Nixon for President" button.

5. A teacher is asked to remove her "Nixon for President" button.

6. The principal tells the newspaper staff they may not print the article criticizing the school lunches.

7. Johnny is told to stop passing out anti-abortion pamphlets in his classes.

8. The "Youth for Hitler" group is not allowed to use school facilities before, during, or after school.

—Day 11—
Privileged and Confidential Communication

Key words/concepts:

confidentiality
Family Education Rights and Privacy Act
professional ethics
professional "need to know"
criminal activity

Scenarios:

1. Diane tells her counselor she can't get along with her parents. The counselor calls the home to find out what's wrong.

2. Bob tells his counselor that he is being ridiculed in class by his science teacher. The counselor speaks to the teacher to hear the other side of the story.

3. Jane tells her P.E. teacher she has been beaten by one of her parents. The teacher calls law enforcement.

4. Joe tells a teacher that he shoplifted some school supplies. The teacher calls the store and sets up an appointment for Joe to meet with the manager.

5. A teacher posts the grades of all students in her classroom to help them identify their missing assignments.

—Day 12—
Student Records

Key words/concepts:

Family Educational Rights and Privacy Act
accurate information

Scenarios:

1. Johnny, a ninth grader, thinks Mr. Williams, the P.E. teacher, put some negative remarks in his file. He is told he can't see the records.

2. His parents ask to see the file and, after reviewing the contents, state that they don't agree with Mr. Williams' comments about Johnny being "lazy" and "a goof-off."

Additional Activities/Resources

1. Peer Practice:

To assist in the learning and understanding of key words and concepts, the strategy of peer tutoring can be used. In this activity, students help each other learn and practice the meanings of terms. It would be best used when an issue has a great number of new words or concepts to associated with it, i.e. freedom of expression.

The teacher needs to prepare two handouts for each pair of students. Each has two columns. Handout A has a list of half of the lesson's terms for the first student to define or explain. The correct definitions are in the right column of Handout B, which the other student holds. Along with the definitions are hints to help the "tutoring" student "tutor" the learner. After going through both sets of terms, papers can be exchanged and repeated.

2. Teams/Games/Tournaments:

This activity was developed at John's Hopkins University as a cooperative learning strategy. Students are divided into **study** groups of four; each group is balanced by sex and ability. Students help each other within this study group to learn a list of 20 to 25 key words concepts.

Study groups then go out to "compete" in a tournament. For the tournament, students are reorganized at tables according to **ability**. Different questions regarding the key words and concepts are chosen at random and asked in turn around the table. A correct answer earns a point for the answering student.

After the tournament, individual points are added for a **study group** total. Rewards are given to the winning groups although each group may win by meeting a previously established criteria for winning (i.e., 20 points out of a possible 25 points.)

3. Poster Project:

Once the constitutional amendments have been studied, groups should choose one each to display on a poster. Words and illustrations should show an understanding and interpretation of the amendments. Posters should be posted, with student permission, for frequent reference.

4. Letter Writing:

Encourage students to write appropriate school or government officials to ask questions or express opinions about rules, laws, or rights.

5. Writing of Class Rules:

A study of rights and responsibilities leads naturally into the writing of rules appropriate for a particular classroom. Start with the Compelling State Interests and then write rules that are compatible in a positive, rather than negative form. ("Be polite" rather than "Don't talk.") Discuss suitable consequences.

6. Visual Aid:

A poster depicting blind justice holding a balance is an example of a useful visual aid. On one side are many students representing the "majority." On the other side is one lone student, representing the individual. The Compelling State Interests may be added to the "majority" side as they are studied; the amendments may be added to the individual side.

7. Guest Speakers:

Invite speakers into the classroom. Possibilities include school officials such as the principal, vice-principal, or superintendent; law enforcement officers; lawyers or judges; members of minority groups to discuss discrimination; someone who has gone to school in a different country; or adults who might speak about going to school in the "good old days."

8. Written Test:

If a final test is used to help evaluate learning, a balance should be found between questions covering rights and those concerning responsibilities. Too often a test on this booklet evaluates students' knowledge of specific rules rather than the concepts of why the rules exist and how they help ensure students' responsibilities and rights. An effort should be made to design questions that will allow students to analyze scenarios, and apply the information to new situations.

Staff Instruction in Judicious Discipline
—By Barbara McEwan—

(The lesson plans that follow were initially developed by Dawn Pierce for use with school bus drivers in the Harpursville, New York, School District. The concepts have here been adapted to assist in the inservice training of all school support staff. These lessons are designed to follow an overview of the concepts of *Judicious Discipline*. The overview should focus on rights balanced against responsibility.)

Session One:
Responsibilities of Support Personnel

Objective:
To review and discuss the responsibilities of school support personnel.

Materials:
Chart paper, markers, paper, pencils, and name tags.

Procedure:
1. Explain to staff members that the purpose of the workshop is to better enable them to work with students in a variety of situations. Discuss the idea that education occurs throughout the school setting and everyone in the school plays a role in helping children understand their citizenship responsibilities. Remind them that they are part of the educational team. They can enhance the learning environment through their modeling and instruction.

2. Ask the staff members to break up into small groups. Choose one person to record what their group discusses concerning staff responsibilities. Include what their responsibilities are and how those responsibilities might change if they are implementing *Judicious Discipline*.

3. Ask the small groups to get back together into a whole group. Ask each group's recorder to read back their list of staff responsibilities. As the recorders are reading their lists, the presenter is writing the items down on chart paper.

4. Review the list and ask if anything else should be added. Are there things that should be deleted?

5. Review with the staff the concept of the balance between rights and Compelling State In-

terests. Discuss which items on the list deal with health and safety, legitimate educational purpose, etc..

6. Have staff members get back into their groups and share with each other real situations that have occurred on their buses, at their work stations, on the playground, or anywhere they encounter students. Ask them to discuss how they might handle problems now, in order to help students practice the concepts of rights balanced against Compelling State Interests.

7. Have the groups share their situations and the proposed solutions with the whole group. Emphasize that *Judicious Discipline* places responsibility for behavior on the students and not the staff, faculty, or administration.

Tell them you will be providing information on consequences in upcoming sessions.

(Following is a sample of a chart listing staff responsibilities. The presenter may want to contribute some of these if the participants don't include them.)

Staff Responsibilities:

1. Safety of the children.

2. Teaching and modeling rights and responsibilities.

3. Teaching and modeling cooperation.

4. Teaching the students correct procedures on the bus, playground, lunch line, etc.

5. Teaching the students correct emergency procedures associated with your duties.

6. Knowing your students.

7. Being fair in dealing with disciplinary problems.

8. Being professional at all times.

9. Greeting students cheerfully to start their day out right.

10. Being conscientious concerning public relations with parents.

[Editor's Note: Along with Compelling State Interests, there are ethical issues listed here. Ethical behavior should certainly be a topic of discussion, if not a complete lesson. At the very least, attention should be called to those items that are better suited under the heading of ethics.]

Session Two:
Responsibilities of Students

Objective:
To review the responsibilities of the students.

Materials:
Chart paper, markers, paper, pencils, and name tags.

Procedure:
1. Review the concept of equal educational ppportunity. Students have a right to attend school and staff members play a very important role in helping to maintain an equitable community within the school. Go on to explain that students also have responsibilities to maintain a safe and healthy environment while they are on the buses, in the cafeteria, on the playground, etc.

2. Review any standing policies for behavior. Discuss how these fall within the Compelling State Interests or how they might be altered to fit more effectively.

3. Ask staff members to break up into small groups, with one person selected to be group recorder. Write down what the groups discusses concerning student responsibilities during the school day. Have them identify the Compelling State Interest involved.

4. After the small groups have completed this task, call them back together for a large group session. Present the concepts of commensurate and compatible consequences. Point out to staff members that it is necessary to think creatively when dealing with discipline situations. The first question should always be "What needs to be learned here?" Avoid developing blanket policies of removing students from buses, the playground, the cafeteria, etc.

5. Ask them to return to their small groups and select a situation from their discussion during the previous lesson. Apply the concepts of commensurate and compatible consequences to the situation. The presenter should circulate to assist the groups in developing consequences.

6. Call the participants back together to discuss the ideas each group developed. Emphasize in closing that all students share a mutual responsibility for appropriate school behavior. Every member of the faculty, staff, and administration of a school should try to work with each student to help assure an equal educational opportunity.

(Following is a brief listing of student responsibilities. The presenter may want to contribute some of these if the participants don't include them.)

Student Responsibilities:

1. Respect the rights and needs of others.

2. Understand that with every right there is a responsibility.

Each school will define the Compelling State Interests in specific language. The responsibility of students is to work within those guidelines. The responsibility of faculty, staff, and administration is to help students understand the guidelines and provide appropriate information when students forget the guidelines.

Wrap-Up Session for Support Staff

Discuss the issues involved in reporting a problem. Who needs to hear about the problem and who does not? Practice strategies for communicating with parents when there is a problem. Make sure support staff understand the chain of command for reporting an incident.

Provide role-playing situations based on actual events from the school. Have support staff role-play their own professional duties as well as the duties of others. Invite participants to offer suggestions on how to respond to difficult situations while adhering to the spirit of *Judicious Discipline*.

Finally, break staff members up into groups representing their own particular function in the school environment. (Bus drivers should work with bus drivers, playground supervisors with playground supervisors, etc.) Have them develop a code of ethics that reflects their special role in the school. Have them record their ethics statement on chart paper. Display the resulting Statements of Ethics prominently in an appropriate site or sites within the school.

Contributors

Margaret Abbott, fourth grade teacher, Wilsonville Elementary School, Wilsonville, Oregon.

Daniel Blaufus, seventh and eighth grade drama and language arts teacher, Kraxberger Middle School, Gladstone, Oregon.

Charlene DeLage, Oregon-based artist with B.F.A. in painting and drawing and M.A. in education from Oregon State University.

Forrest Gathercoal, professor, School of Education, Oregon State University, Corvallis, Oregon, and adjunct professor, Educational Law, Lewis and Clark College, Portland, Oregon.

Paul Gathercoal, assistant professor of education, Gustavus Adolphus College, St. Peter, Minnesota.

Karen M. Higgins, assistant professor, School of Education, Oregon State University, Corvallis, Oregon, and president of the Oregon Council of Teachers of Mathematics.

Richard Jensen, associate professor of education, Western Oregon State College, Monmouth, Oregon.

Rick Knode, social studies , geography, and history teacher, Scappoose High School, Scappoose, Oregon.

Bill Lee, seventh and eighth grade language arts teacher, Cortland Junior/Senior High School, Cortland, New York, and doctoral student at the State University of New York at Binghamton.

Barbara McEwan, associate professor of elementary education, School of Education, Oregon State University, Corvallis, Oregon, and previously a member of the faculty at the State University of New York College at Cortland, New York.

Richard Neuman, high school teacher, Beaverton School District, Beaverton, Oregon.

Betty Powers, fourth grade teacher, Marcellus, New York, and developer and founder of "Reading Right."

Jane Richards, mathematics teacher with the Ithaca City School District, Ithaca, New York.

Thom Thompson, educational consultant, Portland, Oregon, specializing in the area of school and playground safety; he previously served as child development specialist with theVose Elementary School, Beaverton, Oregon.

Juanita Weber-Shirk has served as an ESL teacher in the Ithaca City School District, Ithaca, New York, and was previously employed in various educational programs in Central America.

Heidi Weismuller, first grade teacher in Sauquoit, New York.

Ken Winograd, assistant professor of education, School of Education, Oregon State University, Corvallis, Oregon.

Books about
Judicious Discipline

Judicious Discipline, by Forrest Gathercoal
>   1993 (Third Edition), 220 pp., $14.95
>   ISBN 1-880192-07-1

Judicious Leadership for Residence Hall Living, by Forrest Gathercoal
>   1991, 120 pp., $9.95
>   ISBN 0-9625945-9-8

Judicious Parenting, by Forrest Gathercoal
>   1992, 212 pp., $14.95
>   ISBN 1-880192-03-9

Practicing Judicious Discipline: An Educator's Guide to a Democratic Classroom
>   edited by Barbara McEwan
>   1994 (Second Edition), 128 pp., $14.95
>   ISBN 1-880192-09-8

All of the above books may be ordered from:
>   Caddo Gap Press
>   3145 Geary Boulevard, Suite 275
>   San Francisco, California 94118
>   Telephone - 415/750-9978
>   FAX - 415/668-5450